## Praise for the Football School series

"The hilarious follow-up to the first *Football School* book, packed with even more amazing football facts, cartoons, jokes..."
***The Week Junior***

"Will spark a love of learning in any child who reads it… Intelligent, inspiring, funny…"
***Head of Education, Premier League***

"We love this book series!"
***Match of the Day Weekly***

"A mix of cheeky text and fun cartoons… Perfect for getting kids to pick up a book..."
***The Sun***

"Innovative and entertaining…"
***The Bookseller***

To Oisín, Rohan and Aoife – A.B.

To Sonny, Ollo and G.G. – B.L.

For Kaz, Ethan and Stevie – S.G.

First published 2017 by Walker Books Ltd
87 Vauxhall Walk, London SE11 5HJ

This edition published 2018

2 4 6 8 10 9 7 5 3



This book has been typeset in Palatino

Printed and bound by CPI Group (UK) Ltd, Croydon CR0 4YY



British Library Cataloguing in Publication Data:
a catalogue record for this book is available from the British Library

ISBN 978-1-4063-7921-1

WALKER BOOKS

FSC
www.fsc.org
MIX
Paper from responsible sources
FSC® C020471

www.walker.co.uk

www.footballschool.co

# FOOTBALL SCHOOL

## Season 2

### WHERE FOOTBALL ~~EXPLAINS~~ *Saves* THE WORLD

ALEX BELLOS & BEN LYTTLETON

Illustrated by Spike Gerrell

Welcome to Football School Season 2!
It's great to see you again. I'm Alex.
And I'm Ben. We're your teachers.
Or coaches, because at Football School every lesson is about football.
Our favourite kind of lesson!
We believe you can learn loads about the world through football.
In physics, we'll be expanding our minds with the fact that footballs are not truly round!
In geography, we'll be sniffing around dinosaur poo to discover what it tells us about grass.
And in biology, we will find out whether boys or girls are more likely to be left-footed.
Right!
No, left!
AB
BL

You're going to be amazed by:
The women who were once the most famous footballers in Britain.
And the most awesome stadiums in the world.
In order to find the best football stories we have spoken to loads of brilliant people.
Like the player who speaks EIGHT languages.
And the best mower in the Premier League.
You will also meet our star pupils. They are outstanding in their subjects!
We have a quiz at the end of each lesson. You can be a star pupil too if you get the answers right. We bet you'll get more right than your friends and family.
Extra! Extra! This season we have introduced after school clubs with lots of activities you can do at home.
They will exercise your muscles and your mind.
Because everything at Football School is designed to make you a better footballer.
And a smarter one too!
AB
B

# MEET YOUR COACHES

## ALEX "BELLINHOS" BELLOS

### Coach Stats

Birthplace: Oxford
Height: 5ft 8ins
Colour of hair: Black
Favourite number: 22
Cool fact about home: Can see Wembley Stadium from my window
Favourite school subject: Maths
Favourite book while at school: *The Hobbit*
Keepy-uppy record: 22
Favourite player: Garrincha (Brazil)
Favourite footballers' haircut: Marouane Fellaini (curly and proud of it!)
Favourite goal: Archie Gemmill for Scotland against The Netherlands in the 1978 World Cup
Football dream: Heart of Midlothian win the Champions League

# Coach Stats

**Birthplace:** London
**Height:** 6ft
**Colour of hair:** Brown
**Favourite number:** 8
**Cool fact about home:** There's a park at the end of my road for extra football practice
**Favourite school subject:** English
**Favourite book while at school:** *Treasure Island*
**Keepy-uppy record:** 94
**Favourite player:** Ousmane Dembélé (France)
**Favourite footballers' haircut:** The mullet (short sides, long at back) worn by the 1990s England player Chris Waddle
**Favourite goal:** Antonin Panenka's chipped penalty in 1976 European Championships
**Football dream:** Getting the call-up to play for England

## BEN "THE PEN" LYTTLETON

# TIMETABLE

| | MONDAY | TUESDAY |
|---|---|---|
| REGISTRATION | | |
| LESSON 1<br>LESSON 2 | PSHE<br>10–21 | HISTORY<br>54–65 |
| LESSON 3<br>LESSON 4 | MODERN LANGUAGES<br>22–39 | GEOGRAPHY<br>66–77 |
| LUNCH | | |
| LESSON 5 | PHYSICS<br>40–51 | FILM STUDIES<br>78–91 |
| AFTER SCHOOL CLUB | FEET<br>52–53 | MIND<br>92–93 |

Find the answers to the quizzes on page 206. But no cheating!
BL

Monday
Lesson 1+2

# PSHE

Hello, everyone! It's the beginning of Season 2 at Football School, and we're going to start by revealing a stinky ritual that footballers perform at the beginning of every season.

Professional footballers must provide their clubs with small tubes of their finest pee!

Can you imagine it? Yuck!

But it's true. The players all head to the loo, where each of them piddles into a small container. They hand over the flask of their warm, golden liquid to the team doctors, who test it.

Pee is mostly water, but it also contains small amounts of other substances. Doctors check these substances for health problems like infection, diabetes and disease, which may otherwise go unnoticed.

In this lesson we'll find out what you can learn from your pee. We'll be looking at the water system in our bodies: fluids go in, fluids go out, and fluids go all about.

Are you thirsty for this knowledge?

Drink up!

# WATER WORKS

Water has no colour, no taste and no smell. Sounds like a really boring liquid!

But that's not true. Water keeps us alive. Inside our bodies, water is working non-stop doing all these jobs:

- Making our food mushy so it can pass through our digestive system
- Helping blood and nutrients circulate around our body
- Regulating our body temperature
- Making our joints move smoothly
- Removing waste products in pee

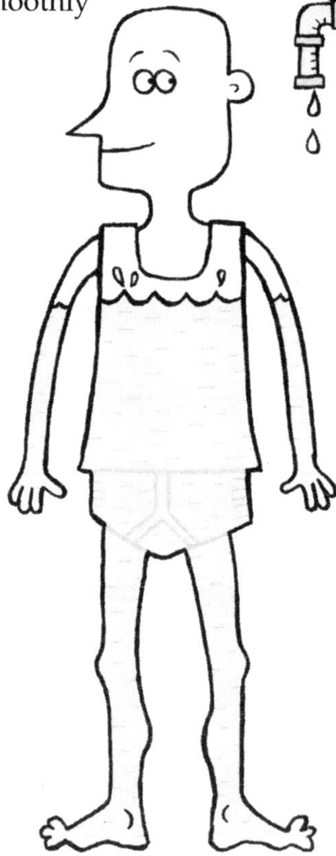

Water does so much for us that we need lots of it. In fact, there is so much water in our bodies that it makes up about 60 per cent of our bodyweight. Humans aren't really flesh and blood. We're mostly water!

A healthy adult can go without food for around a month, providing they are allowed water. (We don't recommend trying it!) But an adult cannot live for more than three or four days without water. Humans need water to survive.

# A SWEATY JOB

Water goes into our bodies in the form of food and drink.

Water leaves our bodies in our pee and sweat. There are also small amounts in our poo and breath. We'll come to pee later, but first here's the juice about sweat.

Sweat is the body's tool for cooling itself down. When the weather is hot or we're exercising, our bodies warm up and we sweat.

Sweat is made up almost entirely of water, with a pinch of salt, which is why it tastes a bit salty. On the surface of our skin are millions of **sweat glands**, which are tiny tubes that produce sweat. When sweat comes out of the glands it appears on the outside of the skin. Once the sweat is on the skin's surface, it starts to disappear into the air, a process called **evaporation**. When the sweat evaporates it takes the heat from your body. And when the body loses heat, it cools down.

The hotter our bodies get, the more we sweat. Everyone sweats different amounts. It depends on things like your build and fitness levels.

Sportspeople sweat a lot. Footballers will sweat between one and two litres during a game, which is equivalent to four to eight glasses of water. In the summer when it is really hot, players can sweat up to four litres, or sixteen glasses of water, which is around 5 per cent of their bodyweight in sweat. Phew!

## WATER LEVELS

If we have the right amount of water in our bodies, we say we are **hydrated**. If we have too little water in our bodies from sweating or not drinking enough, we are **dehydrated**.

It is never good to be dehydrated. It can give you headaches, increase tiredness, make you lose concentration and PUT YOU IN A REALLY BAD MOOD. In fact, you should see Alex when he's dehydrated!

Footballers are careful to avoid dehydration because it affects their game. One team doctor told us that a 5 per cent reduction in the amount of water in a body can result in a 20 per cent drop in performance. On the pitch, dehydration can cause:

- Slower reaction times
- Worse coordination
- Reduced control of the joints
- Increased chance of strains and sprains

To make sure players are properly hydrated, they need to make sure they replace the water lost through sweating. That's why players are often sipping drinks during the stops in play.

## TAKING THE PEE

Back to the other main way our bodies lose water: through the **urinary system**, which makes pee.

The important organs in the urinary system are the **kidneys** and the **bladder**. We are born with two kidneys, although we only need one to be working in order to have a normal life. **Urine**, or pee, is made in the kidneys, and then travels to the bladder via the **ureter**. When the bladder is nearly full, our brain tells us we need to go to the loo. Pee then passes out of the body through the **urethra**.

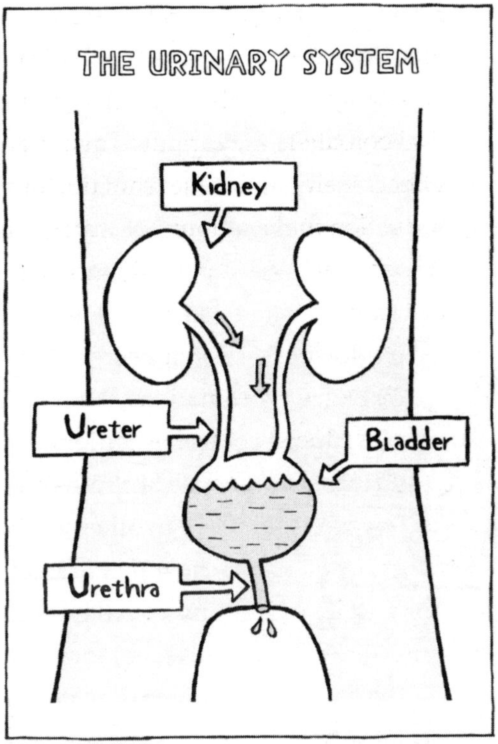

## CLEVER KIDS

The kidneys make sure our bodies contain the right amount of water.

In order to understand how they do this, we need to follow the path of water after it's entered our mouths. First the water flows down into the stomach, then into the intestines where it gets absorbed into our bloodstream.

Here is where the kidneys come in. When blood passes through the kidneys, the kidneys filter the blood and extract water and waste chemicals from it. This water and the waste chemicals eventually become pee.

But our kidneys are smart. If the body is dehydrated, then much of the extracted water is reabsorbed back into the blood. But if the body is well hydrated, the extracted water becomes pee because the body doesn't need it.

In other words, the kidneys decide how much urine to make based on how well hydrated the body is. Clever kidneys!

The colour of your pee depends on how much water the kidneys extract. If a person is properly hydrated, then the kidneys will release lots of water. The pee will be light yellow because the waste chemicals in it have been watered down or **diluted**.

But if a person is dehydrated, the kidneys will not release much water and the pee will be dark yellow or even orangey brown, since the waste chemicals will be much stronger or **concentrated.**

## HOW'S MY PEE?

We visited one professional football club where there is a pee colour chart in the toilets. The chart has lots of shades of yellow, from light to dark.

The players use the colour chart to check that their pee is one of the lighter shades of yellow, which means they are properly hydrated. If their pee is too dark they are dehydrated and need to drink some water.

Next time you go to the loo, look at the colour of your pee. If it is light yellow, you are drinking enough water. If it is dark yellow, you might want to drink a little more today. If it is bright red, you might have been eating beetroot!

## WEE LOVE IT!

Many people around the world drink their own pee. They do so because they believe it is good for their health, and may even cure some diseases, even though there is no scientific proof that this is true. Famous pee-drinkers include a prime minister of India and a world champion boxer from Mexico. Knock out!

## TO PEE OR NOT TO PEE?

As well as water and waste substances, urine can show signs of disease and infection, which is why club doctors check their players' pee. Urine can also contain evidence that footballers have been taking **performance-enhancing drugs**, which are banned.

If you are taking drugs, they get in your bloodstream. The kidneys will extract them and put them in your pee. There's no hiding when it comes to the urinary system.

For this reason, professional footballers are often asked to provide a urine sample at training or straight after a match. The pee police – known as **Doping Control Officers (DCO)** – then check the sample for any banned chemicals.

When a DCO asks a player for a urine sample, the officer must watch the player peeing into the tube, so they know it is fresh pee and not pee they could have stored earlier or got from someone else.

But some people find it very difficult to pee when they are being watched! Players also have to pee a certain amount, so if they have sweated a lot, they will need to drink loads in order to produce their sample, which can result in the player vomiting or peeing all night. One club doctor told us that sometimes players have taken hours to pee, which causes them huge embarrassment, since it can hold up the whole team from travelling home.

# THANKS DAD

Our kidneys are essential to our survival – so it's a good job we have two. If one kidney stops working, you can get by with just the other one. But if both stop working then you will need to have a **kidney transplant**, which is when a healthy kidney is taken from someone else and put into your body. Sometimes a person's body will accept the new kidney, and that person may be able to regain full health. But sometimes the body will reject it, in which case a further transplant is needed.

In 2007, Croatian striker Ivan Klasnić was diagnosed with kidney failure. His mum decided to give him one of her kidneys, but Ivan's body rejected it. Then his father gave him one of his and it worked. Klasnić recovered well enough to play for Croatia at Euro 2008 and scored two goals in the competition, making him the first kidney transplant patient to compete at a major tournament. Sadly, however, his father's kidney stopped working properly in 2016, and Klasnić is now on the waiting list for a third donor.

# URINE GOAL

Argentine goalkeeper Sergio Goycochea had a wee-ird habit before penalty shoot-outs. He would crouch behind the line in his own goal and wee onto the pitch through his shorts. The first time he did it was in the 1990 World Cup quarter-final against Yugoslavia, and he saved two penalties and one hit the crossbar. A few days later he did the same trick in the semi-final against competition host Italy, and he saved two more. "It was my lucky charm," he said.

# PSHE QUIZ

**1. What is the scientific name for pee?**

a) Bile
b) Faeces
c) Mucus
d) Urine

**2. Which part of the body has no sweat glands?**

a) The nose
b) The lips
c) The ears
d) The palms of the hands

**3. The chemical formula for water is $H_20$. What do the H and the O stand for?**

a) Hydrogen and Oxygen
b) Hippo and Octopus
c) Humid and Omnipresent
d) Hazard and Ozil

**4. Which food gives your pee a strong smell?**

a) Asparagus
b) Aubergine
c) Avocado
d) Beetroot

**5. Which of these is correct?**

a) Peeing was a competitive sport in ancient Greece.
b) The ancient Romans used pee to whiten their teeth.
c) The ancient Egyptians used pee as a perfume.
d) Pee soup is an ancient British delicacy.

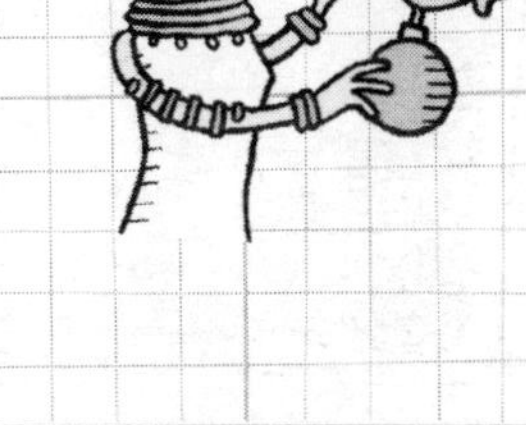

Monday
Lesson 3+4

# MODERN LANGUAGES

Everyone speaks football.

If you go on holiday to another country, it is possible to have a game against the locals even if no one understands a word anyone else is saying.

In fact, it is possible to be on the same football team as someone and not understand a word they are saying. And this happens quite a lot now in professional football. Top teams have players from many different countries who speak many different languages. Sometimes two players may not have a language in common. So if they are together – next to each other at dinner, on the subs' bench or on the team bus – they may not be able to communicate with words at all. When coaches are unable to speak the same language as the players, they will use an interpreter to translate what they are saying in order for their players to understand them. (Eventually players will pick up words of the local language, but learning new words takes time.)

In this lesson we're going to look at why there are so many different languages and how they are created. You'll also learn about chickens in Brazil.

Let's go! *Los geht's! Vamos! Allons-y!*

# SPREAD THE WORD

Most scientists think modern humans originated in Africa within the last 200,000 years. These early groups of people did lots of exploring. It is believed that they and their descendants slowly walked out of Africa and settled all over the world.

Our earliest ancestors probably grunted and squeaked at each other. From these funny noises emerged spoken language, which is a system of words like the ones we use now. One theory is that the first humans to speak all used the same language, but as they moved from Africa around the world, this early language evolved into other languages, which then changed into even more languages. Language is always changing, as speakers replace old words with new words. If you add too many new words to a language, it becomes a different one! The world now has about 7,000 spoken languages.

You can see how much languages change by looking at English over the last few hundred years. Here are some of language expert Mark Forsyth's favourite words that we don't use any more. We love them too – Alex fudgels all the time!

| OLD WORDS | WHEN AND WHERE | MEANING |
|---|---|---|
| Fudgel | 18th century, England | To pretend to work when you're not really |
| Gongoozle | 1940s, England | To stare lazily at a canal and do nothing |
| Groke | 19th century, Scotland | To look at someone who's eating in the hope they will give you some food |
| Snollygoster | 19th century, USA | A dishonest politician |
| Wamblecropt | 16th century, England | To be overcome with indigestion |

And lots of new words – which your great-great-great grandparents would never have heard – have now entered the language:

| NEW WORDS | MEANING |
|---|---|
| Clickbait | A website link that's designed to attract attention and encourage people to read on |
| Emoji | A small image used to express an emotion or idea in electronic communication |
| Olinguito | A racoon-like animal from South America that was discovered in 2013 |
| Squee | A high-pitched squealing sound |
| YOLO | Short for "You Only Live Once", an expression that means you should have fun now and not think about the future |

# SOUNDS THE SAME

In Europe there are about 40 main languages. Many are quite similar to each other. For example, French, Spanish, Portuguese, Italian and Romanian have many words in common because they are all descended from Latin, the language of the ancient Romans. English and German have many similarities, as do Swedish, Norwegian, Danish and Icelandic.

Often countries that are close to each other geographically have similar words for the same thing. This is because people living near each other share and borrow words, just as they might trade goods. For example, consider the word "football". It was first used in English about five hundred years ago.

The game of football didn't exist at that time, so the "football" referred to a "round instrument to play with" using one's foot.

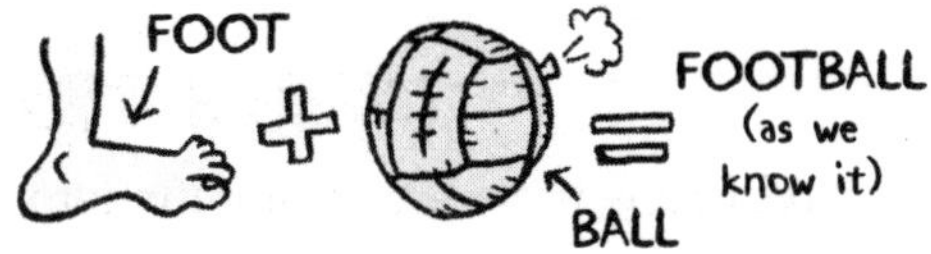


But by the late nineteenth century, "football" meant the game we know and love today. As the game became popular around the world, many different countries started talking about it and introduced the word "football" into their languages. But they changed the word a little bit, so it would fit with their local rules for spelling and pronunciation.

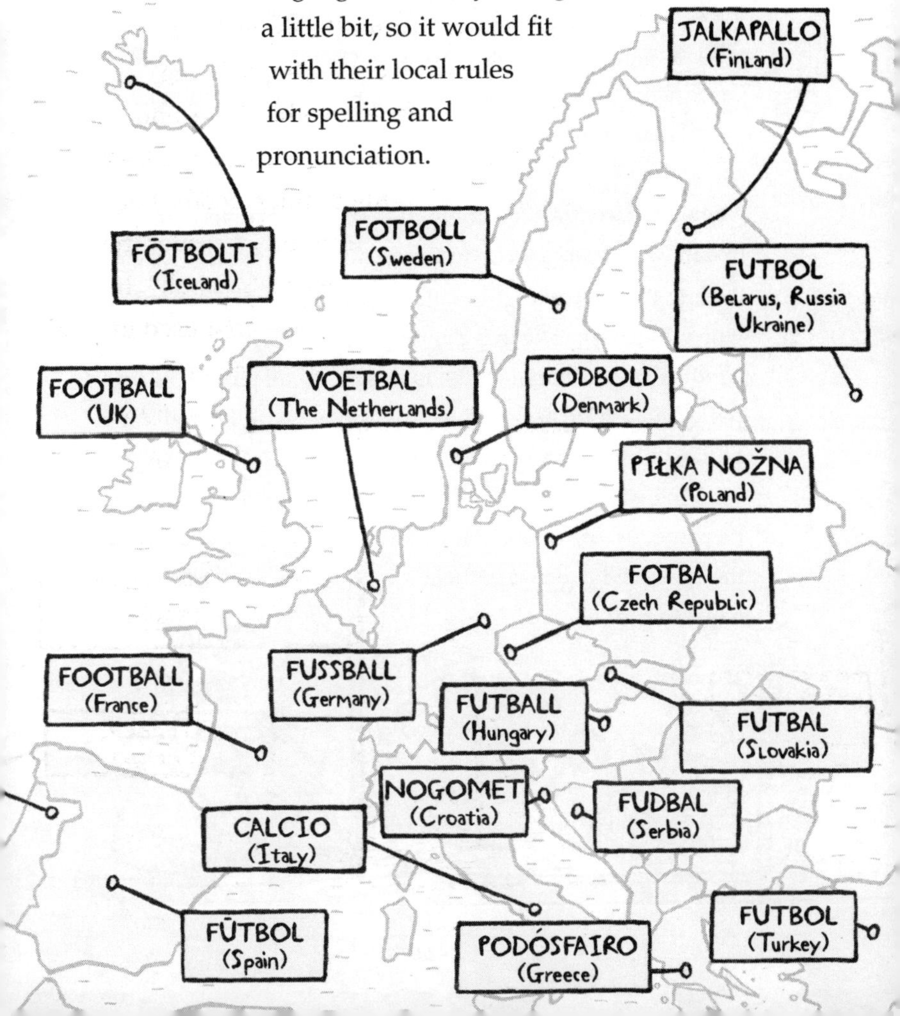

# THE ODDBALLS

As you can see from the map on the previous page, some countries have their own words for football that look nothing like "football". Here are some of the reasons why:

***Calcio* (Italy)**: *Calcio fiorentino* was a violent ball game with 27 players per side, originating in the Italian city of Florence in the sixteenth century. Brits founded Genoa, the first Italian football club, in 1893 but the Italian officials didn't want to use the foreign word "football" to name the sport. So they stuck with *calcio*, from the Italian word *calciare*, meaning to kick. *Calcio fiorentino*, now called *calcio storico* ("historic football"), is still played in summer in Florence.

***Nogomet* (Croatia)**: A combination of the Croatian words *noga* (meaning foot) and *meta* (meaning target). It was coined in the late 1890s by a linguist called Slavko Rutzner-Radmilović, who was eating cake in a Zagreb patisserie when out of the window he saw some students kicking a ball around in a park. The term was used interchangeably with football for a while, but the first football club in Zagreb, PNIŠK, was founded with *nogomet* (and not football) in its name. All other clubs in Croatia then adopted *nogomet* in their name too.

**Soccer (USA)**: In the late nineteenth century, Rugby School in England invented a game with an oval ball that allowed kicking and handling, which they called Rugby football. The other game with the round ball, which was organized by the Football Association, was known as Association football. From Rugby we get the abbreviation "rugger", and from Association we get the word "soccer". For a long time in the UK, the words "football" and "soccer" were used interchangeably, although "soccer" is now hardly used. But in the United States they still say "soccer", since "football" there means what we call American football. Confusing!

***Piłka nożna*** **(Poland)**: The Polish name for football literally means "ball leggy". *Piłka* means ball and *nożna* is a descriptive word, or adjective, which comes from *noga*, meaning leg. It was copied from the English term for football – although incorrectly – shortly after 1900. It became widely used after the first Polish radio broadcast of a football match in 1929.

## TONGUE-TWISTERS

Professional football has become such an international game that players now often move country several times in their careers. Sometimes clubs provide **interpreters** to help players who do not speak the local language. But often footballers learn to speak the lingo. The ones in the table opposite really have the gift of the gab!

Top linguist of his football generation is Croatian midfielder Ivan Rakitić, who as well as speaking EIGHT languages has won La Liga and the Champions League with Barcelona. We interviewed him to find out how he became multi-multi-lingual!

## IVAN, THE TERRIBLY GOOD AT LANGUAGES

**How do you know so many languages, Ivan?**

My parents spoke Croatian, and I grew up in Switzerland, where many languages are spoken. Now my wife is Spanish and we speak Spanish at home! Communication is important in a team, and I've always wanted to learn the language of the club where I am playing, and also speak to team-mates in their home language.

**What is your favourite word?**

Love / amor / ljubav / liebe / amour.

| PLAYER | NUMBER OF LANGUAGES | LANGUAGES |
|---|---|---|
| Ivan Rakitić (Croatia) | 8 | Catalan, Croatian, English, French, German, Italian, Spanish, Swiss-German |
| Mikel Arteta (Spain) | 7 | Basque, Catalan, English, French, Italian, Portuguese, Spanish |
| Gelson Fernandes (Switzerland) | 7 | English, French, German, Italian, Portuguese, Spanish, Swiss-German |
| Philippe Senderos (Switzerland) | 7 | English, French, German, Italian, Serbian, Spanish, Swiss-German |
| Clarence Seedorf (The Netherlands) | 6 | English, Dutch, Italian, Portuguese, Spanish, Surinamese |

**What language do you dream in?**

A mix of all of them!

**Do your team-mates call you "The Dictionary"?**

No, but it is great to be able to speak to people in their mother tongue, especially when they have just arrived at your club. It helps them settle in and feel at home more quickly.

**Will you work as an interpreter when you retire?**

I still have a lot of football to play, so am focused on my playing career, but I hope to work in a job with an international profile requiring several languages and travel once I stop playing.

# WONDERFUL WORLD OF WORDS

Languages need to have words for basic everyday things such as hand, table and sun. But sometimes you get amazing words that only exist in one language. Here are some of our favourites – we wish English had them!

| WORD | LANGUAGE | REGION | MEANING |
|---|---|---|---|
| Abanyawoih-warrgahmarnegan-jginjeng | Bininj Gun-wok | Northern Australia | I cooked the wrong meat for them again |
| Embasan | Maguindanao | Philippines | To take a bath with your clothes on |
| Hanyauku | Rukwangali | Namibia | To walk on warm sand on your tiptoes |
| Ribuytibuy | Mundari | India and Bangladesh | The sound, sight or motion of a big person's buttocks rubbing together as they walk |
| Zhaghzhagh | Persian | Iraq | The chattering of teeth from the cold or from anger |

## WORDS OF HOPE

Here's a tip for players who find learning a second language difficult. Learn Esperanto! It is a language that was invented to be as simple as possible to learn.

Polish doctor Ludwik Zamenhof created Esperanto in 1887. He wanted to make it easier for people of different nationalities to communicate as he thought it would make everyone nicer to each other. He called the language Esperanto – which is Esperanto for "one who hopes".

Many hundreds of thousands of people can speak the language – at least a little bit. And Esperanto even has its own football team, made up of speakers from Argentina, Brazil, Czech Republic, France, Hungary, Nepal, Slovakia, Switzerland and Taiwan.

When it comes to football, different languages often use different phrases to describe what goes on in the game. Turn over for our favourite entries from the *ABCD (EFGH)*, which is short for *Alex and Ben's Classroom Dictionary (Edition For Going on Holiday)*.

## Alex and Ben's Classroom Dictionary

***biscotto*** (Italian for **biscuit**)

- A match which ends in a result that suits both competing teams, usually a drawn game in the group stages of a tournament. The term comes from horse-racing, when horses would be given a biscuit mixed with banned substances – to make them either faster or slower – with the purpose of fixing the outcome.

***cola de vaca*** (Spanish for **cow's tail**)

- A trick that involves stopping the ball and then changing direction. Skilful players like Lionel Messi and Gareth Bale are experts at doing this, often by keeping the ball close to their instep and leaving their marker behind.

***Fahrstuhlmannschaft*** (German for **elevator team**)

- A yo-yo team, describing a side that regularly gets relegated and then promoted.

***brilstand*** (Dutch for **glasses stand**)

- A goalless game, since 0–0 looks like glasses.

**Key** | = tactic | **X** = mistake | = technique | = team talk

***frango*** (Brazilian Portuguese for **chicken**)

• One of the most common phrases used in Brazilian football, it means a goal that is the result of an embarrassing mistake by the goalkeeper. **X**

***jisatsu-ten*** (Japanese for **suicide point**)

• An own goal, dating back to when ancient Japanese warriors, known as samurai, would commit *harakiri*, or kill themselves, rather than suffer the shame of being captured and tortured by enemies. Each player on the pitch takes responsibility for their actions – but they do not die if they score past their own goalkeeper! QO

***hacer un sombrero*** (Spanish for **to make a hat**)

• Chipping the ball over an opponent's head and running around to retrieve it.

***korokoro*** (Japanese for **the sound of something rolling slowly across the ground,** like a heavy wheelbarrow pushed across a field or an acorn rolling into a pond)

- A penalty rolled in slowly to the corner where the goalkeeper does not dive.

***Notbremse*** (German for **emergency brake**)

- A professional foul, when a player deliberately fouls an opponent to prevent a clear goal-scoring opportunity. The punishment is a red card.

***lanterne rouge*** (French for **red lantern**)

- The team at the bottom of the table, named for the last carriage on a train in France which has a red light at the back. The same term is used in German, *rote Laterne.*

***pipoqueiro*** (Brazilian Portuguese for **popcorn-seller**)

- A player who avoids taking risks and doesn't play well in important games.

***saut de grenouille*** (French for **frog jump**)

• When a player keeps the ball between both feet and jumps over the leg of an opponent. In South America it is also known as the *Cuauhteminha*, or Blanco Hop, after the Mexican player Cuauhtemoc Blanco, who pulled off the trick in a 1998 World Cup match against South Korea.

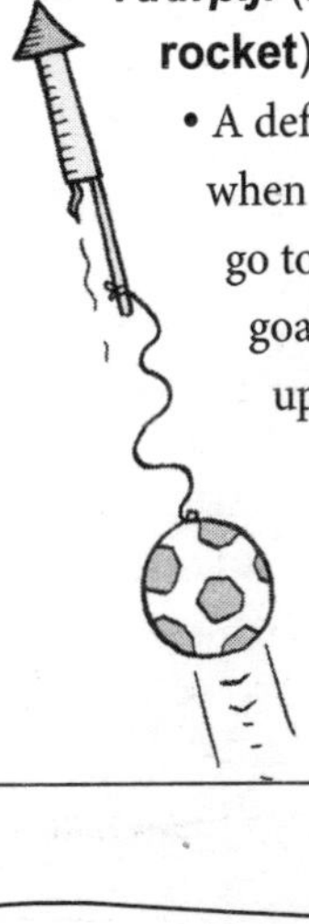

***vuurpijl*** (Dutch for **rocket**)

• A defensive clearance when the ball does not go towards the other goal but is hit straight up into the air.

***zona Cesarini*** (Italian for **last few minutes of a game**)

• Injury time, named after Juventus winger Renato Cesarini, who struck a very late winning goal for Italy against Hungary in 1931. One week later, Ambrosiana-Inter beat Roma with a late goal which led the commentator to refer back to the Cesarini goal. In time, *zona Cesarini* became the popular term for a late goal.

# LINGO BINGO

* There are 7,000 spoken languages today.
* 1 language dies out every fortnight.
* Languages can have anything from 11 to 144 distinctive sounds. English has about 44.
* There are only 3 vowels in Greenlandic.
* There are 121 different sign languages.

## LYNN GO

STAR PUPIL

"Bonas paroli"
(Esperanto for "It's good to talk!")

## STAR PUPIL Stats

Languages spoken: 23
Languages understood: 15
Sign languages learned: 
Sign languages understood: 
Birthplace: Chatsworth, England
Supports: Torquay United (UK)
Fave player: Petr Čech
Trick: Talks a good game

# MODERN LANGUAGES QUIZ

**1. What does Esperanto mean?**

a) I am desperate for the loo.
b) One who hopes
c) I like playing football.
d) One who speaks ten languages

**2. Translate the following emoji into the most likely sentence:**

a) I just swatted a fly.
b) Praise the Lord!
c) Well done!
d) My hands are leaking water.

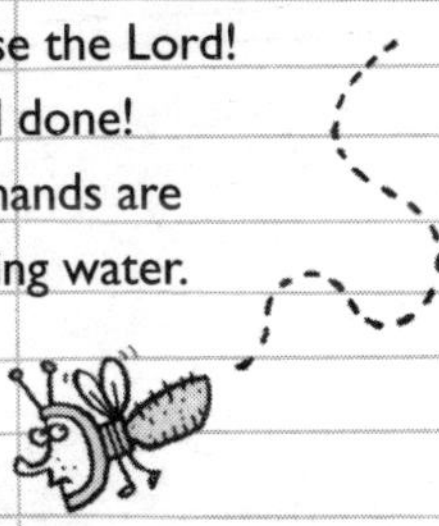

**3. What is the literal translation of the name of Spanish midfielder Juan Mata in English?**

a) John Mates
b) John Matters
c) John Kills
d) John Scores

**4. In German, if you are *fernweh*, you are:**

a) Longing to go to a place far away
b) Full after eating too much food
c) Alone in the woods
d) Always asking too many questions

**5. What is the translation of the Italian word *cucchiaio*, used to describe a penalty that is lofted down the middle of the goal?**

a) Doughnut
b) Gift
c) Spoon
d) Curly pasta

Monday
Lesson 5

# PHYSICS

A ball is round. Simple!

Well, not really. Professional footballs are anything but simple. For a start, they have four parts: **panels of leather** on the outside, a **lining**, a **bladder** inside and a special tube called a **valve**. (You inflate the ball using a pump and a needle that is stuck through the valve.)

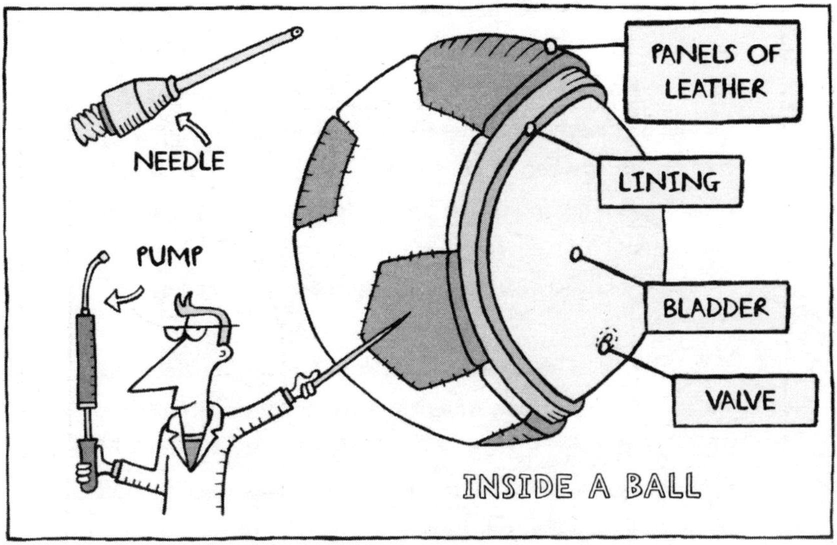


Second, although they may look it, balls are NOT perfectly round. Their surfaces are actually very uneven. They have seams between the panels, and a rough texture on the leather.

In this lesson we are going to take a closer look at the shape of footballs and how they are made to improve play. But first we're going to show you just how far modern balls have come since the time they were made out of pigs' bladders and got so heavy with water it was almost impossible to score a goal from 30 yards away.

Oink oink! Splish splosh!

# ON THE BALL

Here's a round-up of the bounciest facts about balls.

**Pigs will fly:** The first footballs were made from pigs' bladders. Yes, the organ that stores porky pee! Pigs' bladders are light and stretchy and can be inflated with air and then tied, which made them perfectly suited for the job. The bladders were then covered with leather so they would keep their shape and not burst when kicked around. The oldest surviving football in the world is about 500 years old: it was made from cow leather stitched over a pig's bladder and was discovered at Stirling Castle in Scotland.

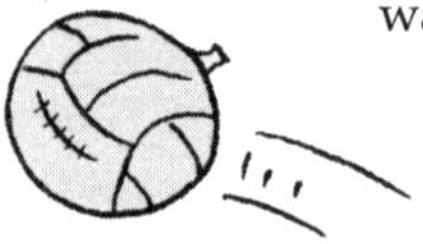

**Good year for balls:** In the mid-nineteenth century, American inventor Charles Goodyear discovered a way to turn latex, a milky substance found in the rubber tree, into hard rubber. In 1855 he made the first football using rubber: it had rubber panels glued at the seams, and was inflated with air. Boing!

**Argie-bargy:** For the 1930 World Cup there was no official ball. South American rivals Uruguay and Argentina faced off in the final and each wanted to use their own ball. FIFA eventually settled the dispute by ruling that the Argentine ball (which was a bit lighter than the Uruguayan ball) would be used in the first half and the Uruguayan ball in the second half. The Argentines won the first half 2–1 with their own ball, but the Uruguayans scored three goals in the second half with their ball, winning the game 4–2. The ball seemed to make all the difference!

**To dye for:** The first leather balls were brown. In the 1950s white balls were introduced so that fans could see the ball in floodlit games. In the 1960s balls were made black and white so they were easier to see on the TV. The Premier League now has three types of ball: a white one for the summer, a high-visibility yellow one for the winter and an orange one for when there is snow.

**Heavy stuff:** Early balls were held together by stitching and had a slit for the valve at the top of the ball that was sewn up with laces. Water could enter the ball through the tiny holes made by the thread, making it heavier and harder to kick. Design improvements to the valve meant that footballs didn't need the laces any more. (Some sports, like American football, kept the laces as part of the ball design because they make throwing the ball easier.) Today the panels on a professional football are held together with a method that bonds them using heat so they are much better protected from absorbing water.

**Wet ball:** Cow leather was once used for the outside panels. Today artificial leather is used, which mimics the feel of leather but absorbs less water. Some balls also have a rough texture to them, which channels the moisture on the surface of the ball so there is more traction when you kick.

# PANEL SHOW

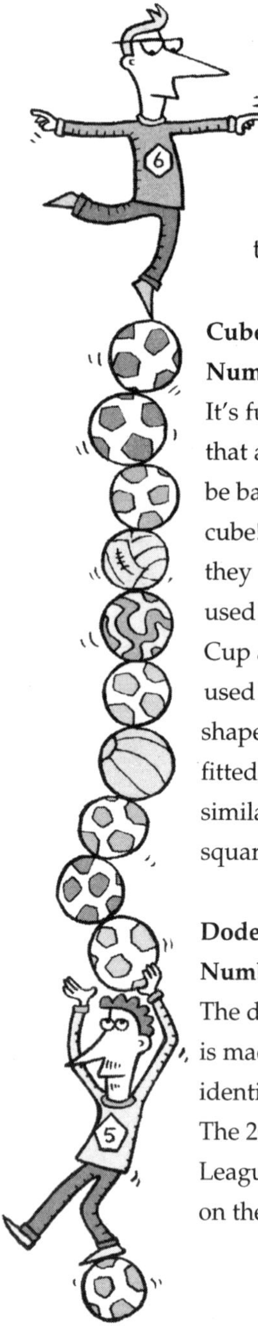

The outside skin of a football is made by attaching identical flat leather panels together. When the ball is inflated with air, the panels stretch into a round ball. Here are the three main ways panels are joined together. Each is based on a geometric shape.

**Cube**
**Number of panels: 6**
It's funny to think that a round ball can be based on a square cube! But it can, and they are! Both balls used in the 2014 World Cup and Euro 2016 used six propeller-shaped panels that fitted together in a similar way to the square faces of a cube.

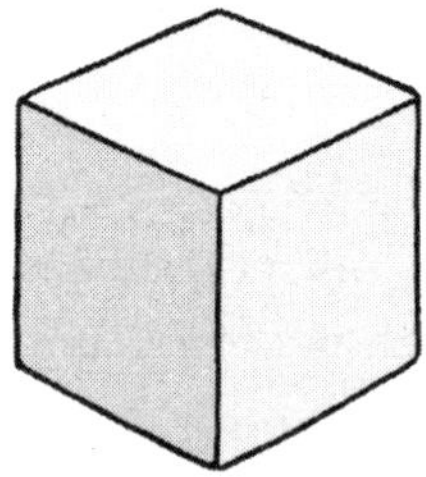

**Dodecahedron**
**Number of panels: 12**
The dodecahedron is made up of twelve identical pentagons. The 2017/18 Premier League ball is based on the dodecahedron.

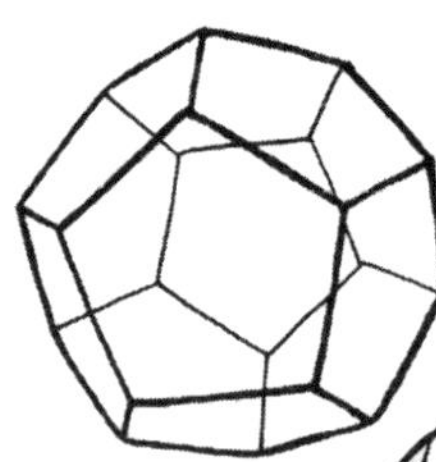

**Truncated icosahedron**
**Number of sides: 32**

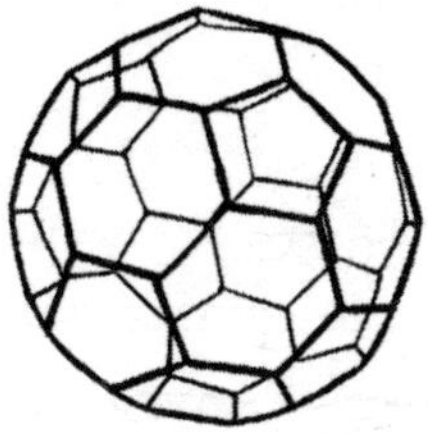

The truncated icosahedron is a shape first studied by the ancient Greek mathematician Archimedes more than 2,000 years ago, but not for playing ball games! It is made up from twenty hexagons and twelve pentagons. The design became a football classic when it was used in the 1970 World Cup.

## GLOBAL GLOBES

These are the World Cup balls from 1970 to 2014:

| YEAR | HOST COUNTRY | BALL NAME |
|---|---|---|
| 1970 | Mexico | Telstar Durlast |
| 1974 | West Germany | Telstar Durlast |
| 1978 | Argentina | Tango Durlast |
| 1982 | Spain | Tango España |
| 1986 | Mexico | Azteca |
| 1990 | Italy | Etrusco Unico |
| 1994 | USA | Questra |
| 1998 | France | Tricolore |
| 2002 | Korea/Japan | Fevernova |
| 2006 | Germany | Teamgeist |
| 2010 | South Africa | Jabulani |
| 2014 | Brazil | Brazuca |

The 1999 Women's World Cup was played with a specially designed ball called the Icon. Since then, the tournament has been played with the Fevernova (2003), Teamgeist (2007), Speedcell (2011) and Conext15 (2015).

## BALL BOOT CAMP

Professional footballers come in all shapes and sizes. But professional footballs must all be the same. Imagine what would happen if the referee showed up with a match ball the size of a pea. Or one as bouncy as a space hopper. In order to make sure that all professional footballs are as similar as possible, FIFA requires that all balls pass the following tests:

**1. Size (Circumference)**

The ball must have a **circumference** of between 68.5cm and 69.5cm. (That's the distance all the way around it.)

**The test:** the ball is put in a machine that measures the circumference at 4,500 different points.

**2. Roundness (Sphericity)**
The ball must not deviate by more than 1.5 per cent from a perfect sphere, which is the technical term for a perfectly round object.
**The test:** the same machine that calculates the circumference also calculates how spherical the ball is.

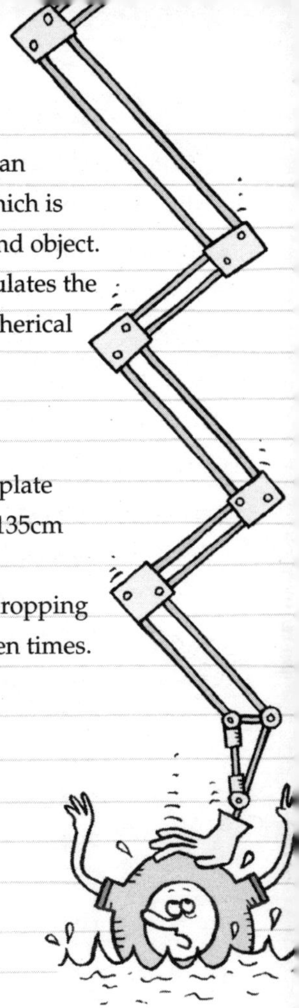

**3. Bounce (Rebound)**
A ball dropped from 2m onto a steel plate must bounce to a height of between 135cm and 155cm.
**The test:** the ball is placed in a ball-dropping machine and the bounce measured ten times.

**4. Water absorption**
Balls must not absorb more than 10 per cent of their weight in water.
**The test:** the ball is placed in a tank full of water. A robotic arm squashes and turns the ball 250 times in the tank, after which the wet ball is weighed.

**5. Weight**

The ball must be between 420g and 445g.

**The test:** the ball is weighed three times in a cabinet protected from the wind.

**6. Loss of pressure**

Balls are firm because the air inside them pushes the sides out. The force being applied by the air across the inside of the ball is called the **air pressure**. The ball's pressure must not decrease by more than 20 per cent over three days.

**The test:** the ball is inflated to standard pressure, and its pressure is measured again after 72 hours.

**7. Shape and size retention**

After being kicked around, the seams and air valve must stay undamaged, the circumference must not change by more than 1.5 per cent, its roundness must not deviate by more than 1.5 per cent and its pressure must not change by more than 0.1 bar (which is the unit of pressure).

**The test:** the ball is measured, then placed in a machine that fires it 2,000 times against a steel plate at 50km per hour, after which it is measured again.

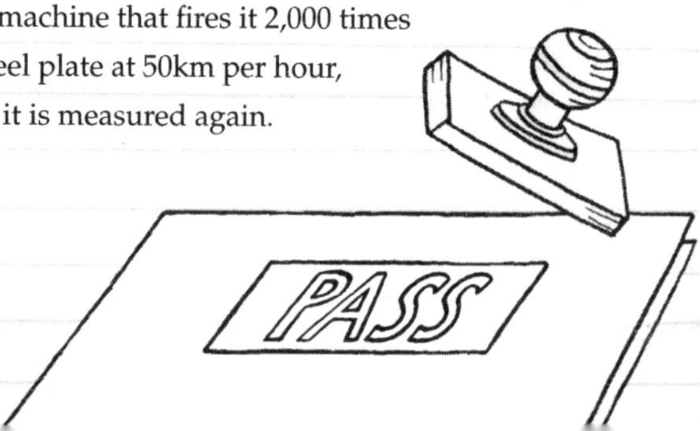

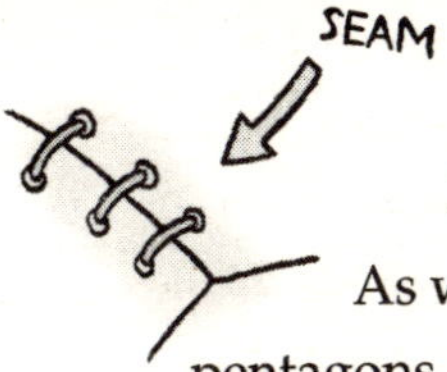


## SEAMS LIKE A NICE BALL

As we saw, the leather panels used on balls can be pentagons, hexagons or propellers. Now let's look at the seams between them. The seams are more than they seem!

The seam helps stop the football from wobbling all over the place. Here's why. The smoothest ball in sport is the ping pong ball. If you have ever played table tennis, you'll know that when you whack the ball it swerves like crazy. This is because the surface of a ping pong ball is very smooth, and the smoother a ball is the less predictable its path will be. That's why golf balls are deliberately made with dimples: the dimples stop the ball wobbling when it is flying through the air.

The same is true of footballs. A perfectly round football would be a nightmare for players and especially keepers, since its path through the air once kicked would be hard to control. The seams in a football stop it veering off-course. In the 2010 World Cup, players complained that the tournament's official ball swerved unpredictably when kicked or headed. An investigation into the ball by scientists revealed that the ball's seams were not as deep as normal balls and this was causing its unpredictability. Whoops!

# INCREDI-BALL!

It's tradition that players who score a hat-trick get to keep the match ball. But what happens if more than one player scores three goals in a game? In that case, the player who completed their hat-trick first keeps the ball. That was a pity for Manchester City players Paul Stewart and David White after they beat Huddersfield 10–1 in 1987. They both scored hat-tricks but so did Tony Adcock, who got three first and walked off with the ball, before it was whisked away and put in the club's trophy cabinet.

# PHYSICS QUIZ

**1. For many years footballs were made using which part of the pig?**

a) Stomach
b) Trotters
c) Buttocks
d) Bladder

**2. Before the beginning of every professional match, what does the referee do to the ball?**

a) Stands on it to make sure it does not burst
b) Kisses it as part of a ritual
c) Checks the air pressure to make sure it is at the correct level
d) Smells it

**3. What happened when a Liverpool fan threw a red beach ball onto the pitch during a 2009 game against Sunderland?**

a) One of the Liverpool players headed the ball into the Sunderland goal
b) The players began an impromptu game of volleyball
c) The Sunderland striker scored a goal when the real ball rebounded off the beach ball past the Liverpool keeper
d) A fan in red swimming trunks and a sunhat ran out to retrieve it

**4. What happened when Switzerland midfielder Valon Behrami tackled France's Antoine Griezmann when the countries met each other at Euro 2016?**

a) The ball burst
b) The ball flew in Behrami's face and knocked him out
c) Behrami hid the ball up his shirt
d) The ball stuck to his boot

**5. The Nike ball used in the 2016/17 Premier League was called the:**

a) Prestige
b) Catalyst
c) Ordem
d) Strike

# FEET FIRST

Football is played with your feet. So, if you want to be good at football, you need to look after them. And we don't just mean stopping them from smelling! You need strong feet for football because when you run, your feet act like levers propelling your entire bodyweight forward. When you receive a ball and control it, your feet behave like flexible shock absorbers.

In the first After School Club of the week, we have four exercises for our feet and ankles that will help toughen up these five-toed trotters. You can even do these in your bedroom, so no excuses. Now, best foot forward!

## Exercise 1: Balancing stick

Stand on a flat surface on one leg with your raised knee bent for 10 seconds. Look at a fixed point on the wall to help you focus. Your arms should be on your hips or by your side. Then do it with your eyes closed. Then switch legs. As you get better, change the surface you're standing on from a flat floor to a sofa cushion, to something wobbly. And when you get good try staying balanced for 30 seconds.

**GOOD FOR: Muscle strength and training the brain**
**DIFFICULTY RATING: 1/4**

### Exercise 2: Heel ordeal

Stand on tiptoes. Hold for 5 seconds, then lower to your heels. Repeat 5 times.

**GOOD FOR: Strengthening muscles at the back of the leg and foot**
**DIFFICULTY RATING: 2/4**

What a bummer!

### Exercise 3: Bum ankles

Put your bare feet together and squat so your bottom touches your ankles. Start by holding the squat for 10 seconds, and then gradually increase to 30 seconds.

**GOOD FOR: General mobility which requires strong ankles**
**DIFFICULTY RATING: 3/4**

### Exercise 4: Toes up

Take off your shoes and socks. Push your big toe down on the floor while pushing the other toes up into the air. No hands allowed! This stretches or flexes your ligaments. Start by holding the stretch for 10 seconds, and then gradually increase to 30 seconds. Don't forget to switch feet.

**GOOD FOR: Pushing off strongly in sprints**
**DIFFICULTY RATING: 4/4**

**FOOT NOTE!** Only do what feels comfortable to you. Do not exceed the stated time in each exercise or you could be at risk of injury.

Tuesday
Lesson 1+2

# HISTORY

Today girls play football at school and dream of becoming professional players and having the chance to win the World Cup.

There are professional women's leagues in countries such as the United States, France, Germany and Sweden. But this was not always the case. Until the final years of the nineteenth century, hardly any women played football.

This was why in 1894 Nettie Honeyball placed a newspaper advert asking for women to join her in founding the British Ladies' Football Club. You might have thought that with a name like Nettie Honeyball, she was destined to love the game! However, Nettie wasn't the woman's real name. She wanted her identity to stay secret, probably because the idea of women's football at that time was so scandalous.

The British Ladies' Football Club lasted only a couple of years. But two decades later, women's football became a phenomenon! In this lesson we are going to look at the moment in history when women's football was more popular than men's football. It happened in Britain at a time when women were demanding the same opportunities as men. At Football School we think women and men should have equal opportunities – on and off the pitch.

# FOOTBALL FACTORY

In 1914 the First World War began. Britain and France were at war with Germany, and in the following years several million British men were sent to fight in France. Soon there weren't enough men in Britain to do lots of essential jobs, particularly physical ones. Traditionally, women were expected to stay at home and look after the children and the house, and do domestic chores like cooking and cleaning. But during the war, women stepped in to help out and took on new roles such as:

- Delivering post
- Factory work
- Farming
- Fishing
- Making weapons
- Teaching in boys' schools

One place that hired lots of women during the First World War was Dick, Kerr and Company, a factory in Lancashire owned by W.B. Dick and John Kerr. The factory usually made trams but during the war switched to making bombs and bullets. The mixture of male and female workers was new for everyone and had an unexpected consequence: one day in 1917 the men challenged the women to a football match.

A football match involving women was an extraordinary idea at that time, since women just didn't play football. But as it was the war and women were doing the same jobs as men, it seemed reasonable that women should join in with football too.

The match was such fun for the women that they decided to carry on playing together. Later that year, they organized a charity football match to raise money for the local hospital that was caring for wounded soldiers. They wanted to play against a team of women, so they asked a group of women at another factory nearby.

The match took place on Christmas Day 1917: Dick, Kerr's Ladies, as they now called themselves, played Arundel Coulthard Foundry. The venue was Deepdale, the stadium of Preston North End, the local professional football team. It had been lying unused because of the war. The match was a huge success. About 10,000 people came to watch and lots of money was raised for the hospital.

## LADIES' GAME

The match sparked a boom in women's football. Dick, Kerr's Ladies began to play more games further afield. They attracted thousands of spectators around the country. Other women's teams started up too. Factory owners were keen for their female workers to play since it boosted spirits and was healthy and cheap entertainment.

Even when the First World War ended on 11 November 1918, women's football continued to spread and Dick, Kerr's Ladies became famous as the best team in the country, rarely losing a match. Their games were always well attended, and in 1919 when Dick, Kerr's travelled to play Newcastle United Ladies, the crowd was 35,000!

Dick, Kerr's players wore the same kit as the men's team – football boots, long socks, shorts and a jersey of black and white vertical stripes – as well as small striped hats to cover their hair. The women quickly became celebrities and an inspiration to countless other women.

On Boxing Day 1920, Dick, Kerr's Ladies played their arch-rivals St Helens Ladies at Goodison Park in Liverpool. The stadium was packed with 53,000 fans and another 14,000 couldn't get in. It was the biggest crowd Liverpool had ever seen. The players needed a police escort to get to the changing rooms.

By now, the Dick, Kerr's Ladies team had a schedule as if they were professional footballers, playing an average of two games a week for nine months of the year. In 1920, Dick, Kerr's Ladies played the first women's international match, against France at Deepdale, in front of a crowd of 25,000. Later that year they played in France. In 1921 alone the team played 67 games.

But they were not professionals, receiving only money for game expenses. In order to get their wages, the women had to work five days a week at the factory and even do a shift before midweek games. They were the hardest-working footballers in the country!

## STADIUM BAN

You might have thought that the success of women's football would be applauded by the Football Association, especially since the games were for charity. But the FA did not like it at all. The women were attracting bigger crowds than the men's professional league, which had restarted in 1919 after the war.

At the end of 1921, the FA passed a ruling saying that clubs were not allowed to use their stadiums for women's football. "The council feel impelled to express their strong opinion that the game of football is quite unsuitable for females and ought not to be encouraged," it said. The ruling was a devastating blow, as it left the women's teams with no decent-sized stadiums to play in. Even though teams like Dick, Kerr's Ladies carried on, only a few fans could watch them play and they were forgotten by the public.

Despite the ruling, in 1922 Dick, Kerr's Ladies went on tour to the United States, playing to crowds of up to 10,000. One newspaper wrote:

> **The Dick, Kerr team is one of the biggest things in soccer to have visited the United States.**

It took until 1971 for the FA to lift its ban on clubs allowing women's football. And since then, women's football has started to grow again with the first Women's World Cup held in 1991.

## WONDER WOMAN

One reason that Dick, Kerr's Ladies almost never lost a match was because they had the best player of that generation. Lily Parr (1905–78) was from St Helens in Merseyside, and learned to play football with her elder brothers. She joined Dick, Kerr's as a winger when she was just fourteen years old – and scored 43 goals in her first season! Parr was famed for her power and aggressive playing style. Six foot tall, she towered over her team-mates. According to one story, she once kicked a ball so hard it broke a male goalkeeper's arm when he tried to catch it.

Parr carried on playing football for Dick, Kerr's Ladies after the FA ban. She continued playing for the team when it later changed its name to Preston Ladies, only retiring in 1951 when her career goal tally stood at more than 900. She is considered the best female footballer of all time and in 2002 was the first woman to be inducted into the English Football Hall of Fame at the National Football Museum.

## ON A PAR WITH LILY

We think these three rank with Lily Parr as the best players of all time:

**Mia Hamm (USA)**
The forward made her debut for the United States aged just fifteen years old and went on to score 158 goals in 275 national team appearances. She won two World Cups and two Olympic gold medals. Hamm co-owns American team Los Angeles and is a board member at Italian club Roma.

**Marta (Brazil)**
The Brazilian forward won five consecutive FIFA World Player of the Year Awards (2006–10) and is the Women's World Cup's all-time leading goal-scorer. She averages more than a goal per game for Brazil – and has played over 100 games!

**Sun Wen (China)**
The former captain of China was voted FIFA's Female Player of the Century after winning four Asian Cups and playing in four World Cups and two Olympics. She was top scorer and best player in the 1999 Women's World Cup.

## EQUAL RIGHTS

When Dick, Kerr's Ladies started playing football, they were showing that women could do something traditionally thought of as just being for men. At that time in history, men and women had very different roles in society. Women were seen mostly as homemakers, staying at home rather than going to work. They raised children, served their husbands and made sure domestic life was well run. Men were out of the house all day and earned the money.

But there were other differences too between the roles and status of men and women. Perhaps the most controversial difference was that only men were allowed to vote at **general elections**, which is when the country chooses the prime minister.

In the years before the First World War, some women were so outraged that they were not allowed to take part in general elections, that they began to campaign for the

right to vote. In 1903, Emmeline Pankhurst founded a movement called the Women's Social and Political Union, one of several that campaigned at this time. Some activists for these movements – known as **suffragettes**, since the word "suffrage" means the right to vote – used violent techniques like smashing windows of public buildings and setting fire to them, and chaining themselves to railings. When they were arrested by the police, they went on hunger strike in prison, meaning they refused to eat.

When the First World War began in 1914, most suffragettes stopped their campaigning in order to help with the war effort. In 1918, the same year the war ended, the government gave the vote to women over the age of 30, in part thanks to the vital role women played during the war by taking over men's roles. A decade later, in 1928, the government lowered the voting age for women to twenty-one, which is what it was at that time for men. Since then men and women have had equal voting rights in the UK.

# SHE'S IN CHARGE

More than 50 countries have now had women as their elected leaders, including:

| COUNTRY | LEADER | POSITION | DATES |
|---|---|---|---|
| Argentina | Cristina Kirchner | President | 2007–15 |
| Australia | Julia Gillard | Prime Minister | 2010–13 |
| Brazil | Dilma Rousseff | President | 2011–16 |
| Germany | Angela Merkel | Chancellor | from 2005 |
| India | Indira Gandhi | Prime Minister | 1966–77, 1980–84 |
| United Kingdom | Margaret Thatcher | Prime Minister | 1979–90 |
| United Kingdom | Theresa May | Prime Minister | from 2016 |

# HISTORY QUIZ

**1. During the First World War, why did women start to do many of the jobs traditionally done by men?**

a) Because women are better than men
b) Because many men had joined the army to fight
c) Because men wanted companionship at work
d) Because women got better marks in their exams

**2. If you play football, but do not get paid for it, what type of player are you?**

a) Rubbish
b) Semi-professional
c) Poor
d) Amateur

**3. What is a foundry?**

a) A factory that casts metal
b) A factory that uses material found on the street
c) A place where you go to dry clothes
d) A cheese shop

**4. Who were the suffragettes?**

a) Women who campaigned for the right to vote in elections
b) Female fans from Suffolk
c) The name given to the female supporters of a losing team
d) A girl band

**5. Which team has won the Women's World Cup most times?**

a) Germany
b) Japan
c) Norway
d) USA

Tuesday
Lesson 3+4

# GEOGRAPHY

Pitches have changed in many ways since 1863, when the rules of football were first written down:

- The maximum length of a pitch used to be 183 metres. Today it is 105 metres.
- Originally there were no markings for the penalty spot, the penalty box, the D, the halfway line and the centre circle.
- Goals used to be just two upright posts. Then a tape was hung between the posts. Later a crossbar was introduced, and later still a net was added to avoid doubt over scored goals.

One thing, however, has stayed the same: the surface of the pitch. Football has always been played on grass.

In this lesson we are going to discover why grass is one of the most amazing plants in the world. Not only is grass crucial to football and many other sports, it has also changed the course of civilization.

Weed on!

# GRASS IS CLASS

Grass is one of the oldest types of plant. Scientists think it was growing around 100 million years ago, during the age of the dinosaurs, because they found five types of grass in a dinosaur's fossilized poo. Stinky business!

- All grasses have similar characteristics. They all have a hollow stem and usually leaves, or blades, which are long and thin and relatively rigid. Some grass leaves are so sharp they can cut human skin.
- Grass comes in many varieties. There are about 10,000 different species, including short grass that we use on lawns and long grass that grows higher than a house.
- Grasses are long-lived. Some species of grass can live for hundreds of years.
- Grass is versatile. It will grow on pretty much every habitat on Earth, including hot deserts, rainforests and cold mountains.
- Grass is everywhere! You will find it on all the world's continents, even Antarctica. In fact, up to 40 per cent of all the land in the world is covered in grass.

## GRAZE CRAZE

Some of the most common foods we eat are grasses, such as wheat, maize, rice and oats. We eat the seeds of these grasses, which we call **grains**. In fact, the discovery that we could grow grasses for their grains was the moment that humans stopped being hunter-gatherers, moving from place to place, looking for food. Instead we became farmers, based in the same place, tending our fields and storing grains for use all year round. This was the beginning of villages, towns and eventually cities.

Animals like cows, horses, sheep and deer are grass-eaters too. In fact, the word "graze", which we use to describe how these animals eat, means to eat grass.

This means that grass is an important food for humans in two ways. First, as something for us to eat, and second as something for the animals that we eat to eat. The process by which plants (such as grass) are eaten by animals (such as cows) which in turn are eaten by other animals (such as humans) is called a **food chain**.

### MULTI-GRASSING

Bread comes from wheat, which is a grass, and sugar comes from sugar cane, which is also a grass. So if you are having a sandwich and some orange squash while watching a football match, you are eating, drinking and watching grass at the same time!

## ONE MAN WENT TO MOW...

Grass isn't just for eating. In the form of lawns, it has become an essential part of people's gardens. Ben loves mowing the lawn at the weekend, although his lines tend to be a bit wonky. Alex's are much straighter! The first lawns were grassy fields that surrounded English castles, which were kept short, either by cattle grazing on them or by workmen who used sharp-bladed tools called scythes. The grass had to be kept short so enemies could be spotted approaching the castle.

By the 1800s having a grass lawn around your house had become a sign of wealth, because you could only have a lawn on your land if you were able to pay workmen to cut it with scythes. Using a scythe was slow and laborious work, and a big lawn required a team of scythe-wielding men. Expensive!

But all this changed thanks to Edwin Beard Budding, an inventor who was asked by a clothing factory to find a way of cutting off all the tufty bits of cloth from soldiers' uniforms. He invented a machine with a rotating device that cut off the tufts. He realized his invention could work on grass ... and in 1830 he invented the lawnmower.

The lawnmower made it cheaper and easier to maintain a lawn. The Budding Mower became a bestseller, and changed our gardens forever.

## ...WENT TO MOW A MEADOW

One of the loudest songs sung at Chelsea matches is the children's nursery rhyme "One Man Went to Mow". Fans think it was introduced by a Chelsea fan called Mickey Greenaway, who played a nursery rhyme tape of the song while Chelsea were playing a friendly match in Sweden in 1981. Chelsea fans all sang along and eventually the chant made it back to Stamford Bridge.

## SPORTING PLANTS

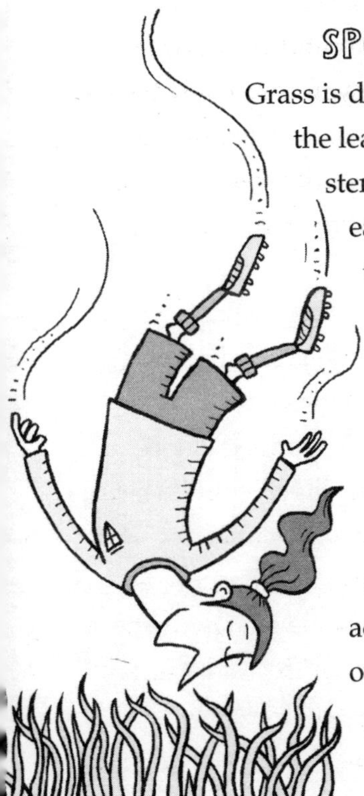

Grass is different from other plants because the leaves grow from the bottom of the stem. This means it can withstand being eaten from the top and also being trampled on. It is this resistance that makes it perfect for football pitches. Unlike other plants, it doesn't die when it's stamped on.

Even though the blades of some grasses can be really sharp, other species are very soft. Softer grasses are ideal for sport as the plant will act as a cushion when players fall over. Even the best artificial football pitches are not as soft as a well-tended grass pitch.

# TURF WAR

Just as English castle-owners hired people to maintain their lawns, so do football clubs. Football pitches require a lot of attention to be at their best. We wanted to find out more, so we visited a club with a cutting-edge reputation and the man who has helped make it.

Leicester City surprised everyone when they won the 2015/16 Premier League title. It wasn't the only award they took home that season though: because of the brilliant pitch at their King Power Stadium and the pitches at their training-ground, the club won Professional Football Grounds Team of the Year. We can only imagine the shear delight at the club! The grounds team celebrated by mowing diamond shapes into the pitch on the final day of the season, with a star inside each diamond. It was a perfectly symmetrical pattern and celebrated the Foxes' double success in style. "It was like drawing a big dot-to-dot picture," the head grounds manager, John Ledwidge, told us.

Leicester have become well-known in football for their original pitch patterns. On Remembrance

Sunday in November 2016, an image of a poppy was mowed into the pitch. But the team lost 2–1, so they might not want to remember it now!

Ledwidge wanted to mow an image of the Champions League ball into the centre circle before European matches, but was forbidden by UEFA, the European governing body. They say that for Champions League games the grass has to be mowed in straight lines. Ledwidge is always coming up with wacky design ideas. He might even mow the Football School crest into our pitch if we ask nicely!

## GREEN FINGERS

Ledwidge's skill is in creating patterns even though grass is just one colour: green. He can shade the green by mowing the grass in different directions: grass bent away from the mower will appear lighter and grass bent towards the mower will appear darker. He gets deeper contrasts between the greens by using a roller which flattens the grass even more. "We try to be as creative as we can within the framework of only using dark green and light green," he says. "We are all mad scientists really!"

In order to create the perfect pitch, every day Ledwidge puts a stick called a moisture probe around fifteen centimetres under the surface to check moisture levels. The probe contains sensors that tell him how much water the grass needs that day. In other words, he is asking the grass how thirsty it is.

Every month, he also takes soil samples to check the levels of nutrients. So he's asking how hungry the grass is! Ledwidge then creates a special mixture, based on what he discovers, to spray on the grass.

In summer the grass needs more water to keep it hydrated – just like a player – while in winter it needs **nutrients** like iron and potassium to strengthen it. Ledwidge even adds liquefied sugar and seaweed to the spray to keep the grass healthy. Apparently Manchester City put garlic in their grass spray. Not good if a team of vampires ever play there!

## LEDWIDGE'S GREAT GRASS FACTS

# PITCH PERFECT

We see the grass on top of the pitch, but this is what's happening below it:

GRASS
25MM
For playing football on!

SYNTHETIC GRASS
180MM
Fake grass made of synthetic fibres is stitched into a mixture of sand and soil. This helps bind the grass roots.

PURE SAND
200MM
To help drainage and prevent waterlogging, as the water moves down from the grass to the roots.

GRAVEL CARPET
Where the pipes for draining away the water are kept.

## HOW DOES YOUR GARDEN GROW?

The length of grass on a pitch or sports field depends on what you want the object in the sport to do. For example, in rugby the ball does not touch the ground, so the grass will be longer than in other sports. Some sports need even longer grass:

| SPORTS PITCH | GRASS LENGTH (MM) |
|---|---|
| Cricket wicket | 0 |
| Golf putting green | 2–3 |
| Bowling green | 4.5 |
| Tennis court | 8–12 |
| Football pitch | 25–30 |
| Rugby pitch | 30–50 |
| Horse racing track | 60+ |

# GEOGRAPHY QUIZ

**1. What grass-related song do Chelsea fans sing?**

a) "The Green Green Grass of Home"
b) "One Man Went to Mow"
c) "Green Grass Grows all Around"
d) "How Does the Grass Grow?"

**2. Why is grass green?**

a) It's not. It's blue!
b) The sun paints it green every night
c) So grasshoppers can jump around without being seen
d) Grass produces a pigment called chlorophyll, which reflects green light

**3. Rotting plants are eaten by flies, which are eaten by spiders, which are eaten by mice, which are eaten by foxes. But what might eat a fox in this food chain?**

a) Duck-billed platypus
b) A fly
c) A unicorn
d) A bear

**4. Which country's league introduced a rule in 2016 saying the grass needed to be greener in order to appeal more to fans and sponsors?**

a) Spain
b) Russia
c) China
d) Greenland

**5. What was unique about the lawnmower that English lower-league club Forest Green Rovers started using in 2012?**

a) The players built it from scratch
b) It was solar powered and used by a robot
c) The manager's 8-year-old son was hired to mow the pitch
d) It painted pitch markings at the same time

Tuesday
Lesson 5
FILM STUDIES
Why are camera operators like great strikers?
Fast forward!
BL
Because they never miss a shot.
Rewind! Replay!
BL

Which team usually gets to the stadium the day before a football match?

The TV crew!

When we sit down in front of the telly to watch a big match, we expect to see every important moment. We want to see every goal from different angles. We also want to see close-ups of the players' and managers' faces, as well as wide shots of the whole team. That's a lot of work for a TV crew.

In fact, a 90-minute televised game is in many ways like a 90-minute film you see at the cinema. They are both full of dazzling and dramatic images, in glorious colour and high definition, and they both need a lot of technical preparation.

In today's lesson, we're going to learn how a game of football is filmed for television.

Lights! Camera! Action!

## WHAT A RIG-MAROLE

Here's a list of the basic equipment a television company needs to televise a football match:

- TV cameras
- Cables
- TV screens
- Computers
- A truck

A truck?! Yes! You'll see why very soon.

All the cameras, cables and computers usually arrive at the stadium the day before the game, together with a team of about 30 people. These include **riggers**, whose job is to set up the equipment, and a team of technical specialists who make sure everything is working properly.

That's right. The TV cameras are not owned by the club or kept in the stadium. They must be set up by the TV company from scratch each time.

The riggers put the cameras in their correct positions around the pitch. They then connect cables between each camera and the truck, which is parked in the stadium car park. The truck opens up to become a TV studio, containing

screens and computers for the technical team who will control the **broadcast** of the game on television.

It takes at least three hours to fully set up and check the equipment. Sometimes it can take up to twelve hours. It's an exhausting day and the match hasn't even started!

## COLOUR BALANCE

One of the crucial jobs on the day before the game is to make sure the cameras are all seeing the same colours. If you ever take several pictures of the same thing from different angles, such as, say, a pair of red socks, you will notice that the red can look totally different in each image. This is because the light is different in each picture.

The same thing happens with TV cameras in a football stadium – the green of the pitch will look different under different lights. Since the lighting will change for every camera position, each of the cameras needs to have its **colour balance** adjusted so they are all the same. It would look very strange if one camera showed the grass as dark green, another as lime green and another as olive green.

## YES WE CAM

This is a camera plan for a typical big game.

You'll notice that almost all the main cameras are on one side of the pitch. That's because the viewer needs to always be clear which team is playing in which direction. If a team is playing from left to right, the images need to show them

### CAMERA PLAN

#### GANTRY CAMERAS

1. CAMERA 1: The main camera, on the halfway line, which provides 60 to 70 per cent of all images. Gives a wide view of the game.
2. CAMERA 2: Next to Camera 1, but used for close-up shots.
3. & 4. 18-YARD CAMERAS: In line with the edge of the box. Both of these cameras are useful for checking offside calls.

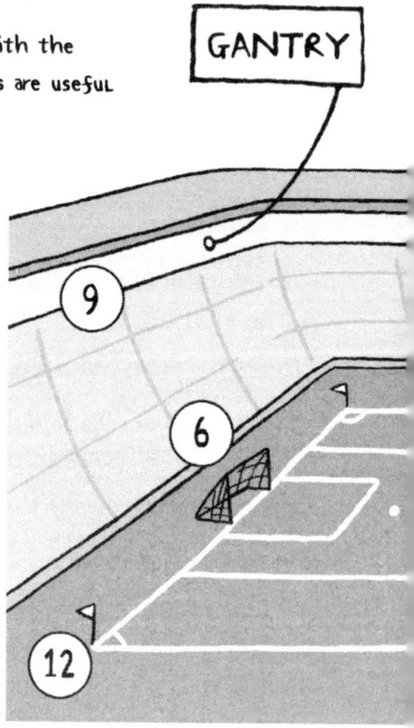


#### PITCHSIDE CAMERAS

5. CAMERA 3: Used for player and referee close ups. When a player is fouled, Camera 3 will shoot the player on the ground, while Camera 2 will shoot the player who committed the foul.
6. & 7. 6-YARD CAMERAS: In line with the box markings, for getting goalmouth action.

playing from left to right. A camera on the opposite side would have them playing right to left, which would be very confusing for the viewer!

Each camera below is operated by someone – some are right up close to the action, and some are high up at the back of the stands on a metal walkway called a **gantry**.

SIDE AND STAND CAMERAS

8. MANAGER CAM: Watching the coaches and the dugout.
9. & 10. HIGH BEHIND GOAL CAMERAS
11. & 12. CORNER CAMERAS: These give you extra angles for replays.
13. BEAUTY CAM: A wide-angle camera that is used to get a beautiful shot of the stadium (perhaps with the sun setting).

## ON THE MOVE

The cameras in the diagram are the cameras that are fixed in one location. But TV companies use other cameras too – ones that move around.

### STEADY ON

If you want to film the teams as they walk out from the dressing room onto the pitch, you need to walk with them. If you want close-up shots of players celebrating on the pitch as soon as the final whistle blows, you need to be as close as possible to them. In both of these situations, the film crew use a **Steadicam**.

A Steadicam is a portable camera that you carry using a special harness. You often see Steadicam operators running around in the middle of the action: the camera is on a stick, which is connected to an arm, which is connected to the harness.

Camera operators need a harness to hold the camera because the equipment is heavy and the harness spreads the weight evenly across their back, shoulders and hips, helping keep the camera as steady as possible when they move.

If you have ever tried to film something on a phone or a camera, you'll know that you have to keep your hands as still as possible, since there's nothing worse than images from a shaky camera. Steadicams are designed to stop camera wobble. Think about what happens when you try

to walk while holding a glass of water full to the brim. In order to stop the water from spilling, you must constantly adjust your arm so that it absorbs the bounce of your walk. Steadicams work on the same principle: the equipment is like a robot arm that will absorb the bounce of your walk, and will keep the camera steady and moving in a fluid motion.

It takes about 40 minutes for a Steadicam operator to get ready, which is mostly spent making sure the weight of the camera and equipment is perfectly balanced on the harness. Altogether the kit weighs 25 kilograms – about the same as a large dog!

Steadicam operators always have an assistant beside them. The Steadicam operator uses one hand to control the direction of the camera, and the other hand to adjust the zoom. The assistant controls the focus, using a dial on a handset. And the assistant also makes sure the operator doesn't accidentally bump into anyone behind them. Eek!

## DRONE ON

Some televised games use a **Batcam**, which is a remote-controlled camera fixed to a **drone**, a remote-controlled flying machine with four propellers. The Batcam hovers above the stadium to get bird's-eye views. The Batcam needs two people to operate it: one for the drone (who must have a drone flying licence) and one for the camera.

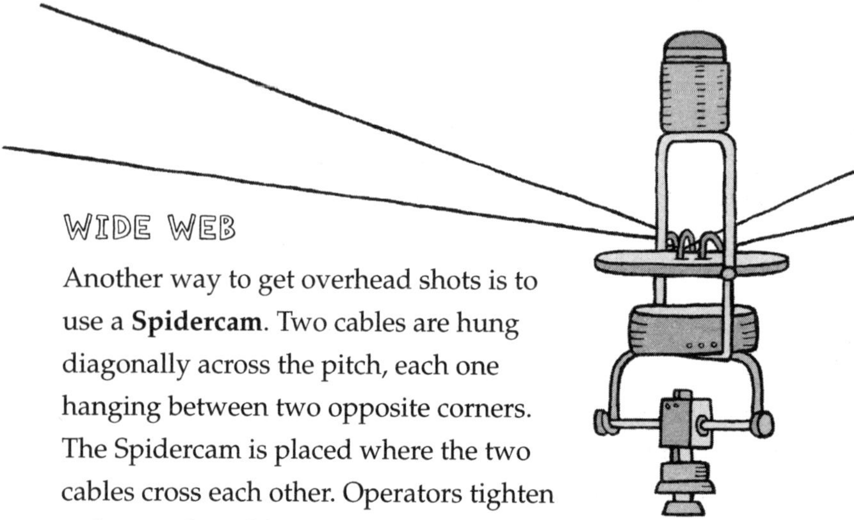

## WIDE WEB

Another way to get overhead shots is to use a **Spidercam**. Two cables are hung diagonally across the pitch, each one hanging between two opposite corners. The Spidercam is placed where the two cables cross each other. Operators tighten or loosen the cables at the four corners of the pitch, and make the Spidercam move in three directions: lengthwise across the pitch, widthwise across the pitch, and higher or lower to cover the action from different heights.

## MEANWHILE, IN THE CAR PARK

The stadium car park does not sound like a particularly interesting place to be while a match is going on, but in fact it is a hive of excitement and activity.

The truck we mentioned earlier has been transformed into a TV studio, full of screens and computers, with space inside for about 20 people.

The most important person in the truck is the **director**, who is sitting in front of a wall of screens that show all the images coming in from the cameras.

The director's job is to choose which of these images is used in the broadcast. Most of the time, the image used will be the overview given by the main camera, Camera 1. But the director needs to be aware of the images coming from all the cameras, in case there is a better view of the action at any moment.

The director wears headphones and a microphone, which are connected to all the camera operators. Often the director talks to the camera operators, asking them to get certain shots.

Also in the truck are other members of the broadcast team, such as the people looking after the sound, the graphics and the replays. Film crews have lots of special words that no one else uses or understands, such as an "aston", which is the term for a caption used on the lower third of the screen, and has nothing to do with Aston Villa!

## ONE MORE TIME

One reason why sports like football are so popular on TV is because of the ability to show replays. We love reliving the best moments again and again. But the first viewers to ever see an instant replay in sports were not so happy. The replay was shown on a channel in the United States in 1963 during a game of American football. When one team scored a touchdown, the channel replayed the moment and the announcer had to make clear that the team were not scoring again. Many viewers were confused and called the channel to complain!

## UNPUNCTUAL GERMANS

The first match of the Bundesliga – the German top division – took place in August 1963. Borussia Dortmund were playing Werder Bremen. Only one TV camera was in the stadium. But the cameraman arrived late and when Dortmund striker Friedhelm Konietzka scored after only 35 seconds, no one was there to film it. This means there is no footage of the first ever Bundesliga goal. Embarrassing, *ja*!

## DON'T MISS IT

When England captain Steven Gerrard scored in his team's 2010 World Cup opening match against the United States, the whole country celebrated. Except, that is, for the thousands of people who missed the goal because one of the TV channels that was showing the game cut to a car advert by mistake. Oops!

The channel had made the same mistake one year earlier, switching to ads with two minutes of extra time left to play of a goalless FA Cup tie between Everton and Liverpool. While viewers were watching an ad for mints, Everton scored a last-minute winner. But all viewers saw was the players celebrating afterwards.

# KE-OWWWWWW-N

Often TV pundits and presenters stand on the side of the pitch before matches and set the scene for the game ahead. One former player was in for a nasty surprise while assessing the pre-match form of Leeds and Arsenal before an FA Cup tie in 2012. A ball from the pitch smashed him on the head while he was chatting on live TV. Ouch!

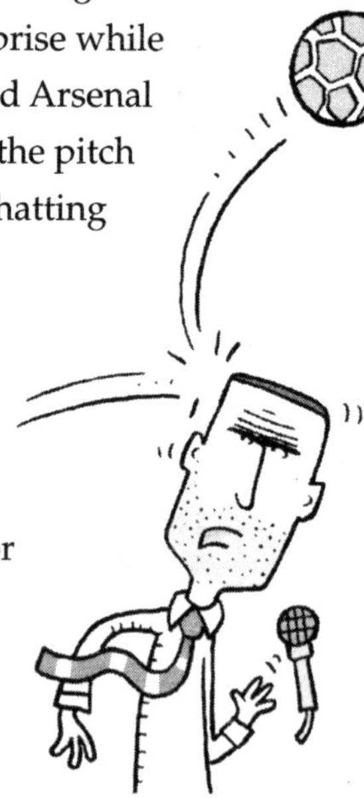

The victim, Martin Keown, a former Arsenal defender, did not look pleased. Keown later claimed that the shot had been struck by Leeds midfielder Michael Brown – who had once played for Arsenal's rivals Spurs – and that Brown had apparently been aiming for the man standing next to Keown, Robbie Savage!

# FILM STUDIES QUIZ

**1. What is the name of the raised platform where the main cameras are placed?**

a) The garret
b) The gantry
c) The pantry
d) The tree

**2. The first match broadcast live on TV was on 16 September 1937. The match was between:**

a) Arsenal and Arsenal Reserves
b) Manchester United and Liverpool
c) England and Scotland
d) Brazil and Argentina

**3. Who decides which pictures will be used on TV?**

a) The producer
b) The director
c) The decider
d) The viewer

**4. In 2013, Argentine footballer Ezequiel Lavezzi, playing for Paris Saint-Germain, walked off the pitch after a hard-fought match against rivals Marseille. What prank did he play on the Steadicam operator?**

a) Slapped him on the bum
b) Tickled him
c) Kissed him
d) Tripped him up

**5. There are about 7.5 billion people in the world. How many of them watched at least a minute of the 2014 World Cup final between Germany and Argentina on TV?**

a) About half a billion
b) About one billion
c) About two billion
d) About three billion

MIND AFTER SCHOOL CLUB

# BRAIN GAME

It's a World Cup final. The world is watching and your team has a penalty that could win the trophy. The captain gives you the ball to take the penalty. What happens next? Will you stay calm, or let your nerves get the better of you? We all face moments of pressure in our lives, whether it's performing in public or taking a test. Footballers are no different. In our second After School Club, we have some ways to mentally prepare you for your next tough challenge. Focus!

## Challenge 1: Knees up

When you get dressed in the morning, tie your shoelaces while standing on one leg. Not only is this task good for muscles and balance, it is also good for coping with mental pressure. We are not used to standing on one leg, so this challenge helps us get comfortable with being uncomfortable. If we are not afraid of being uncomfortable, we are likely to perform much better when the heat is on!

**GOOD FOR: Keeping cool under pressure**
**TIME COMMITMENT: 1/3**

## Challenge 2: Brilliant me

Get a piece of paper and write down all the times you did well at school or in sport, or helped out at home. Also write down nice things that teachers, friends and family members have said to you. Put it somewhere safe. This document will help you feel good about yourself. If you ever have a bad day, look at the piece of paper to remind yourself of all your successes. In sport and in life it is important to believe in yourself. Players who have self-belief will keep trying to succeed even if they sometimes fail.

---

**GOOD FOR: Recovering from setbacks**
**TIME COMMITMENT: 2/3**

## Challenge 3: Check it out

Memorize this checklist.
This list was written by a football psychologist for players, to ensure they are continually progressing in their careers. That's because the best players never think they know everything. The same goes for your teachers and even the Football School coaches. We are always learning! The checklist is a useful reminder of ways to make progress both on and off the pitch.

---

**GOOD FOR: Staying motivated**
**TIME COMMITMENT: 3/3**

Wednesday
Lesson 1+2

# DESIGN AND TECHNOLOGY

Stadiums are buildings where football matches take place in front of spectators. But, of course, they are much more than that! They are often enormous, towering structures that dominate the skylines of their cities. In fact, we think they are a bit like modern-day castles. A stadium, like a castle, strikes fear into the hearts of enemies. A stadium prominently displays its club colours, just like a castle displays flags. And let's not forget the army of fans who treat the stadium as a home and protect its honour by waving banners and scarves and cheering at every match. The most famous stadiums, such as Wembley in London, San Siro in Milan and Camp Nou in Barcelona, are known throughout the world.

In this lesson we are going to find out how stadiums are built so both the players and fans get the most out of a game. We're going to visit some amazing structures and discover some naughty tricks home teams use to upset the visiting team.

But first, something sick.

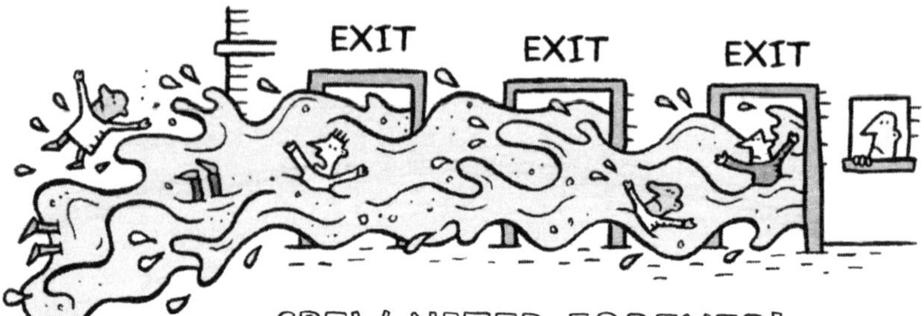


## SPEW-NITED FOREVER!

Heave. Wretch. Gag. Throw up. Puke. Vomit. There are many ways to describe what happens when half-digested food rises up spontaneously and uncontrollably from your stomach. All of a sudden, yucky stuff is going the wrong way up your tubes and out of your mouth. (And sometimes your nose!)

The way vomit gushes out of your body is just like the movement of fans out of a stadium at the end of a game. Think about it. During the match everyone in the stadium is watching the action. That's like having a settled stomach. Then the final whistle blows and everyone leaves at the same time. That's like throwing up. Huge crowds of people spew into the corridors behind the seating area, and these rivers of people slowly move through the stadium until they reach outside.

You may think we are being silly comparing fans to vomit. But we are deadly serious! In fact, the people who design and build stadiums make the same comparison. The corridors that you walk through when you enter or leave a stadium are called **vomitories**. That's the technical term – we promise! It's also Alex's favourite word in this book. (Ben's is *ribuytibuy* – check out Modern Languages to find out why.) Remember, the vomitory is not a place where you go to be sick. It is a place where the movement of people through it resembles the act of vomiting.

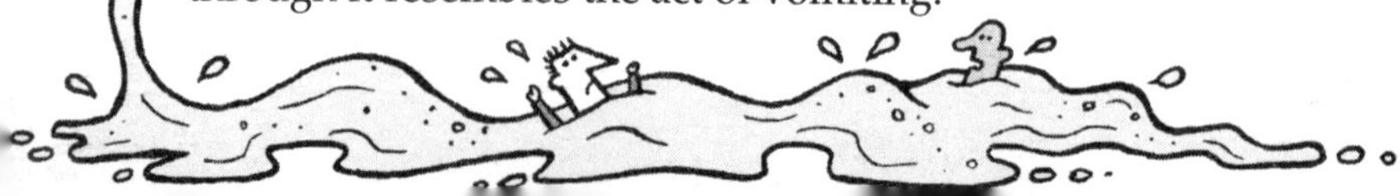

# CROWD CONTROL

If you have ever visited a stadium, you'll know that walking through a vomitory at the end of a match can be a bit scary. You will be in a crowd of thousands of people, who are all moving the same way at the same time. There is no way to go faster. There is no way to go backwards. There is nothing you can do to escape. All you can do is walk slowly in the same direction as everyone else.

Because of the risks of fans causing a stampede, or a crush, as they leave the stadium, **architects**, the people who design and plan buildings, say that the vomitories are one of the most crucial parts of stadium design. If the corridors are too narrow you will get squashed. But if they are too big then you are wasting space that could be used for things that fans need, such as toilets, and things that make the club money, such as food stalls.

Safety guidelines in the UK require stadiums to be designed so that it is possible to get everyone out of the stands in eight minutes. That's not a lot of time to get around 60,000 people out. Sometimes it takes Ben longer than that to get out of bed in the morning!

# ANY SPARE TICKETS?

Most major stadiums are built to hold tens of thousands of fans. But when safety regulations were less strict, some matches attracted more than a hundred thousand spectators, which is about equal to the population of a medium-sized town! Here are the highest confirmed attendances from our favourite moments in football history:

**173,580**

**Stadium:** Maracanã, Rio de Janeiro, Brazil
A world-record crowd was left heartbroken as Brazil lost 2–1 to Uruguay in the 1950 World Cup final. Unofficial estimates claim this attendance might have topped 200,000.

**147,365**

**Stadium:** Hampden Park, Glasgow, Scotland
Fans poured into Scotland's biggest stadium at the time to see Celtic beat Aberdeen 2–1 in the 1937 Scottish Cup final.

**128,000**

**Stadium:** Azadi, Tehran, Iran
Iran drew 1–1 with Australia in the 1998 World Cup qualifying play-off in front of a packed home crowd. Iran ended up qualifying for its first World Cup since 1978.

**126,047**

**Stadium:** Wembley, London, England
Bolton Wanderers beat West Ham United 2–0 in the 1923 FA Cup final, the first ever official match at Wembley. But it's remembered for a grey horse called Billie shepherding the crowds to safety.

## STAND UP, SIT DOWN

The section of the stadium where spectators watch the game is called the **stand**, which is totally confusing since spectators nowadays spend most of the time in the stand sitting down. Go figure!

An architect's job when designing the stand is to give as many people as possible a good view of the action on the pitch. The reason why stadiums are all different is that architects have several other factors to take into account, such as how much money there is to build it, how many people the stadium needs to hold, how many hospitality suites for entertaining VIPs the club wants, and what other uses it might have besides hosting football matches (such as music concerts or other sports games).

Even so, some rules of stadium design are universal. In theatres, cinemas and stadiums, the further back you go from the stage or screen or pitch, the higher the rows of seats get. They have to. Otherwise the back of the head of the person in front of you would be blocking the view.

In modern stadiums, the way the rows get higher follows a mathematical curve called a **parabola**. In this diagram of a cross-section of a stand, you can see that further from the pitch, the rows are higher. Funnily enough, when a football is kicked through the air it also follows a parabola, but one which is upside down and smaller.

You can't carry on the parabola forever because UK safety rules state that the angle between rows must be no greater than 34 degrees.

It's a good idea to have the front row of seats as close to the pitch as possible so the fans are close to the action. One trick to do this, which is used at Arsenal's Emirates Stadium, is to have spectators enter the stand from the top and then walk down, so there are no entrances taking up space at the bottom of the stand.

As well as the vomitories and the stand, another crucial part of the stadium is the roof. In hot countries a roof is needed so fans are protected from the sun. In the UK, fans need to be protected from the rain!

In older stadiums the roofs usually have support pillars to hold them up, but this is not ideal because the pillars obstruct some people's view. Thanks to advances in engineering science, however, it is now possible to design a roof that doesn't need support pillars in the stands – but you need to be very clever. "The most complicated part of stadium design is definitely the roof," a stadium engineer told us. "The roof of a stadium is like a bridge that is a quarter of a kilometre long. The pillars need to be well out of the way."

The requirement to have a roof that doesn't get in the way of spectators has led to some amazing, innovative stadium designs. At Wembley, for example, a gigantic arch 133 metres high and 315 metres wide helps support the roof. Wembley's arch is so big it can be seen right across London. In fact, it is twice as high and 50 per cent wider than London's Tower Bridge.

# HOUSES OF FUN

Here is a whistle-stop tour of some of our favourite stadiums from around the world. Make sure you catch a game at one of these if you can!

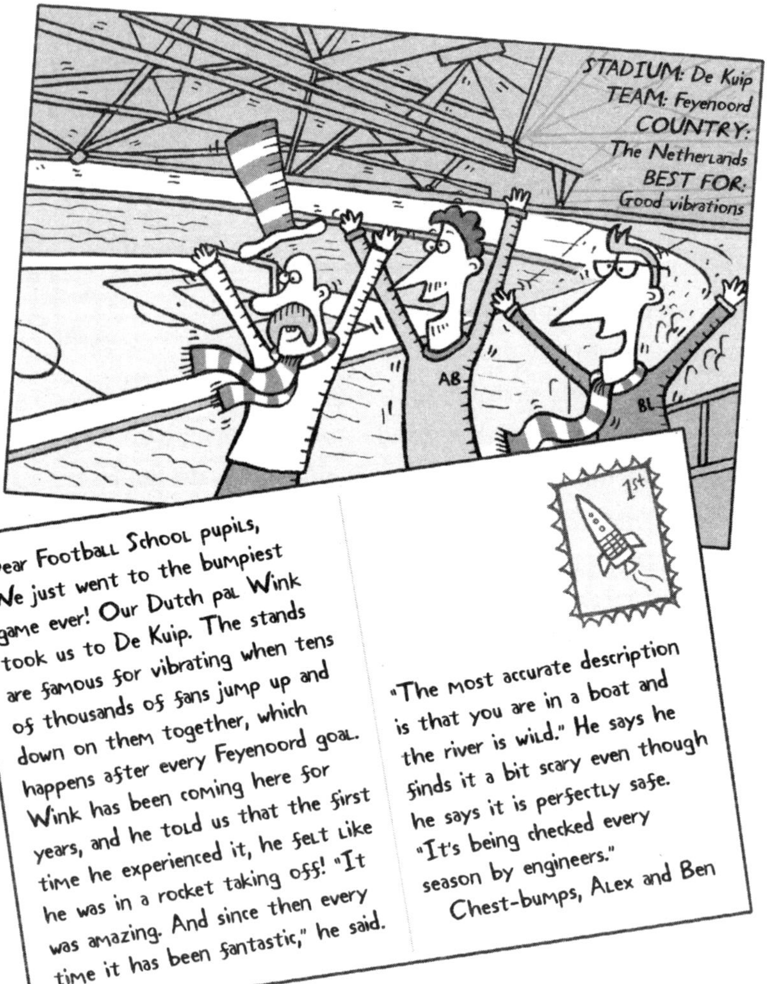

Alex, meu amigo,
I'm watching a match played halfway up a mountain! Behind one of the goals is a sheer rock face that rises higher than the stadium – hence the name "pedreira", which means quarry in Portuguese. I dig it! There are stands for 30,000 spectators on only two sides of the pitch, and behind the other goal is a dramatic

view across Braga and the surrounding countryside.
Cod and hugs, Ben

Lieber Ben!
This awesome stadium is enclosed in a shell made from diamond-shaped panels that light up in any colour. For Bayern Munich games the stadium is red, for 1860 Munich games it is blue and for the German national team it is white.

Shine on,
Alex

STADIUM: The Float at Marina Bay
TEAM: none
COUNTRY: Singapore
BEST FOR: Sea breezes

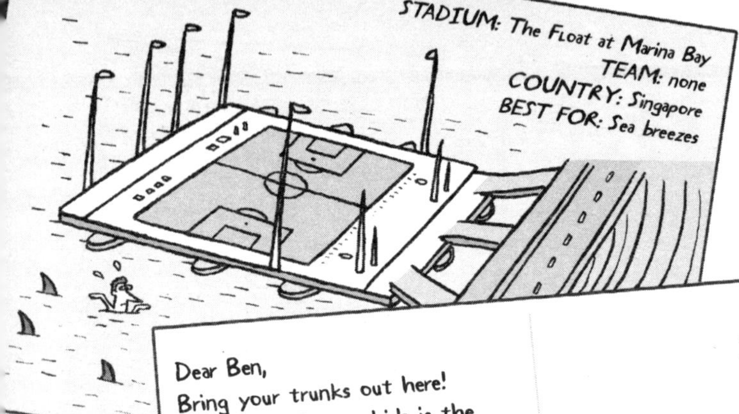

Dear Ben,
Bring your trunks out here! I'm at the Float, which is the world's largest floating stage, made entirely out of steel, and is located in Singapore's Marina Bay. You walk onto it along ramps from the mainland. There is a 30,000-seater stand on the mainland facing the stage, which gives a view of it from only one side. Turf was laid on the stage for a football match in 2008. So far that has been the only match played here! They hope more will happen in the future.

It floats my boat,
Alex

STADIUM: Borisov Arena
TEAM: BATE Borisov, Belarus national team
COUNTRY: Belarus
BEST FOR: Blowing bubbles

Dear Alex,
Are you dotty for stadiums? Then you will love the Borisov Arena! Its silvery shell is full of large, splodge-shaped holes, which makes it look like massive bubbles are rising from the ground. It could be the skeleton of a giant alien. It's spot on!

See you around
(and around and around),
Ben

STADIUM: Timsah (or "Crocodile") Arena
TEAM: Bursaspor
COUNTRY: Turkey
BEST FOR: Snappy dressers

Dear Spike,

Check out this tail! We are in Bursa, Turkey's fourth biggest city, and the local club Bursaspor is building a new stadium. The club is known as the Green Crocodiles and they have decided to build the stadium in the shape of a giant green crocodile! A massive crocodile's head will stick out of the side of the stadium, making

the stands look like the croc's body and tail curled up. Work started in 2011 and is due to finish soon.

Bitey-bye bye!
Alex and Ben

ALEX BELLOS
NEAR WEMBLEY
LONDON
UNITED
KINGDOM

## THEATRE OF CHOCOLATE

Every stadium has its own character and personality. Here are some with the best nicknames:

| STADIUM | TEAM | NICKNAME |
|---|---|---|
| Beijing National Stadium | 2008 Olympic football final | The Bird's Nest |
| Estadio Alberto J. Armando | Boca Juniors (Argentina) | La Bombonera (The Chocolate Box) |
| Old Trafford | Manchester United (England) | The Theatre of Dreams |
| San Mamés | Athletic Bilbao (Spain) | La Catedral (The Cathedral) |
| Stade Geoffroy-Guichard | Saint-Étienne (France) | Le Chaudron (The Cauldron) |

## MIND GAMES

Some clubs play naughty tricks in their home stadium to annoy the visiting team, in the hope that it will make their opponents play badly. We can't be sure which of these pranks have actually been used, since no team is going to fess up to such dastardly plans! But we've heard rumours of all of them (and no, before you ask, we wouldn't let any of these happen at Football School).

- Turning up the radiators to maximum so the visitors feel uncomfortable
- Turning off the water supply so they can't wash and prepare themselves properly

- Painting the walls such a disgusting colour combination that the players feel cold and ill

- Putting pictures of home fans looking angry on all the walls, so the visitors feel scared
- Polishing the floor so thoroughly that visiting players are at risk of slipping up on it, making sure they have to tiptoe as they walk

- Making the changing room as small as possible
- Filling the room with obstacles, such as a table in the middle that means the visiting coach can't talk to all his team at once
- Putting mirrors on walls that are designed to make players look smaller than they are

# SHARING IS CARING

Some teams would never dream of being so naughty. These teams all share their stadiums with their local rivals!

| STADIUM | LOCATION | TEAM |
|---|---|---|
| Ajinomoto | Tokyo, Japan | Tokyo, Tokyo Verdy |
| Allianz Arena | Munich, Germany | Bayern Munich, 1860 Munich |
| Azadi | Tehran, Iran | Esteghlal, Persepolis |
| Maracanã | Rio de Janeiro, Brazil | Flamengo, Fluminense |
| San Siro | Milan, Italy | AC Milan, Inter Milan |
| Stadio Olimpico | Rome, Italy | Lazio, Roma |
| Teddy | Jersualem, Israel | Beitar Jerusalem, Hapoel Jerusalem |
| Tele2 Arena | Stockholm, Sweden | Djurgårdens, Hammarby |

# DESIGN AND TECHNOLOGY QUIZ

**1. What do you do in a vomitory?**

a) vomit
b) cough
c) sneeze
d) walk

**2. The seats in a stadium are in the:**

a) lie
b) kneel
c) sit
d) stand

**3. What architectural feature was also Wembley's nickname before the old stadium was demolished and a new one built in its place?**

a) The Gigantic Slide
b) The Twin Towers
c) The Pyramid Pitch
d) The Golden Arches

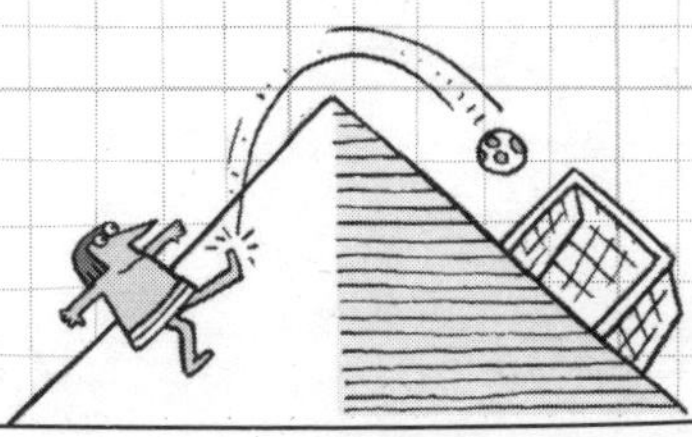

**4. When building a stadium, safety rules say you must build one toilet per roughly how many people?**

a) 10
b) 50
c) 100
d) 500

**5. What is special about the Big Zero stadium in Macapá, Brazil?**

a) It is incredibly small and used by ants
b) Zero big clubs call it their home ground
c) The halfway line runs across the Equator so each half is in a different hemisphere
d) Alex opened the stadium with Pelé and kicked the first ever ball there

Wednesday
Lesson 3+4
ENGLISH
I'm thinking of writing a story. But I can't decide whether to set it in the past, the present or the future.
Sounds tense...
I love grammar so much!
Not as much as me!

Here's a simple tale:

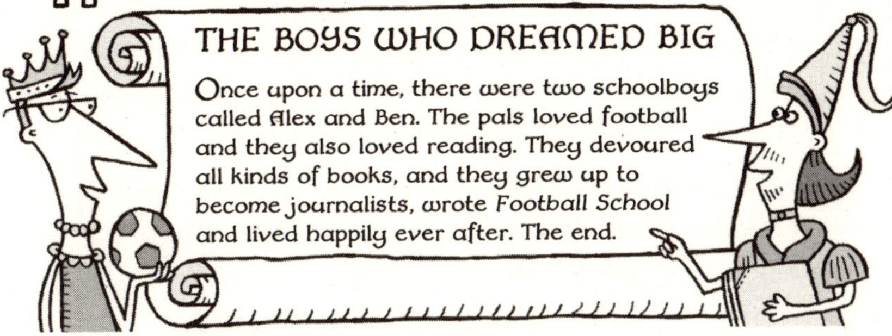


Here's another way to write the same story:

**FOOTBALL TIMES**

**BEST BUDDIES WRITE BALL BOOK**

Two footie friends have come out with a book about the beautiful game. *Football School* is written by Alex and Ben, two journalists who loved reading when they were kids.

The first version is written in the style of a fairy tale and the second in the style of a news report. Fairy tales often start with the words "once upon a time". They are written in a way that creates a sense of magic and wonder. The aim of a news report, however, is to tell the facts in as short and clear a way as possible. No magic allowed!

There are many other ways to tell stories, and we will see some of them in this lesson. But the writing style we will be looking at in most detail is **match reporting**. This is the style used to write about football matches in newspapers and on websites.

Sharpen your pencils, we're ready to go!

## REPORTING BACKWARDS

A **match report** is an article that tells you the story of a football match. If you open the sports pages of a newspaper or look on a sports website you will see many match reports.

The first rule of match reporting is that you start with the end. That might sound strange, but just think about it. What's the first thing you want to know about a match? What the coach had for breakfast? Who was in the line-ups? Whether it was raining when the teams kicked off? No – the first thing you want to know when you read a match report is who won! A match reporter will always write down the name of the winning team in the first sentence of the report.

This technique of starting with the end is very different from many other ways of telling stories. In a fairy tale, for example, you start at the beginning and it is only at the end that you find out how things turn out. You don't start the story of *Little Red Riding Hood* by telling your reader that the Big Bad Wolf is killed.

But in the opening few lines of a match report, you must include a **summary**, or overview, of the main points of the game. This would include the winner, the final score and the name of the goal-scorers. It might also mention any other important incidents, such as a sending off.

We're going to take you through how you would begin a report of the most famous game in English football history. Can you see how all the important parts of the game have been summarized in the opening sentence? The report then continues by discussing key moments or talking points:

## FOOTBALL TIMES

### ENGLAND WIN 1966 WORLD CUP

Geoff Hurst scored a dramatic hat-trick as England beat West Germany 4–2 to win the World Cup for the first time.

Germany had levelled the scores at 2–2 with the last kick of the regular 90 minutes, but England went ahead in extra time thanks to a shot from Hurst, which rebounded off the crossbar and onto the goal line. It was ruled to have crossed the line before bouncing out.

As Germany looked to equalize, England captain Bobby Moore passed to Hurst, who scored a stunning final goal.

Match reports are written in the **third person**, which means that you describe the players as "him", "her", or "them", not as "me" or "you". The choice of words must be kept simple, so the reports are easy to read. And they have many **verbs**, which are words that describe actions. Football matches have a lot of action! "Scored", "beat", "levelled" and "crossed" are all verbs.

Further into the report, you might mention less important moments in the game. You can include background information like the line-ups, the weather and, if it is relevant, maybe even what the coach had for breakfast! A report ends with a **conclusion**, a final few sentences that give an overall perspective on the game:

> As soon as the referee blew the final whistle, fans ran onto the pitch to salute their heroes. The greatest moment in the history of English football was complete.

By the end of the report your reader should have a sense of what really happened in the game. A good match report will explain the game's key moments, best players and whether the result was fair or not.

## TWO SIDES OF THE STORY

Let's take a moment to talk about fairness.

England fans were very happy when the referee judged that Geoff Hurst's controversial shot, which rebounded down after hitting the crossbar, had crossed the goal line before bouncing back into play. But what about the German fans? They were not so happy, as you can imagine!

Think about how a German match reporter would have written up the same game. Can you see how this report is different to the one we just looked at?

**FUSSBALL ZEITUNG**

**WEST GERMANY ROBBED OF 1966 WORLD CUP**

West Germany were unlucky to lose a controversial match 4–2 after one of England's goals was allowed even though the ball did not fully cross the line.

Just like the first match report, the important information, such as who won the match and the final score, is in the opening sentence. But this time the focus is on West Germany losing the game rather than on England winning. For the Germans the key incident of the match was the controversial goal, not the hat-trick by Geoff Hurst.

The rest of a German match report might go like this:

**West Germany had taken an early lead when Helmut Haller scored after 12 minutes, but they needed Wolfgang Weber to equalize with the last kick of the regular 90 minutes.**

**Swiss referee Gottfried Dienst's decision in extra time that Hurst's shot had bounced over the goal line after hitting the crossbar was costly for West Germany. It was controversial as Dienst could not see the incident and couldn't speak the same language as the linesman from Azerbaijan. The West German side will feel that the referee helped England win the game. Without a doubt, Hurst's goal will be debated for decades.**

The English and the German reports make for very different reading, even though they are both talking about the same game.

This is because the match reporters took different decisions about what they thought was important in the game. They made these decisions because they were writing for different audiences.

Football is full of incidents that divide opinion like this. This is what makes it fun to watch – and it also keeps match reporters on their toes!

# A DAY IN THE LIFE OF A MATCH REPORTER

A match reporter has to send in a report as soon as the final whistle blows. This is so people can read the story online the moment the game finishes. How do you write a story so quickly? Ben used to write match reports, so he can explain the tricks of the trade.

## BEN'S MATCH DAY DIARY

**13:00** My editor tells me how many words I need to write – it could be up to 1,000 words.

**14:00** I arrive at the stadium and pick up my ticket.

**14:15** I eat. All Premier League clubs provide meals for the press.

**14:45** I go to the press box, the section of the stand reserved for journalists. It has the best view: usually near the halfway line so you can see both goals. The seats have desks and little TVs that show replays.

**15:00** The game begins! I watch about 30 minutes before I start typing. I describe any goals or exciting incidents. It's hard to type and follow the game, but the crowd noise is a good indicator of when to pay attention.

**15:45** By half-time I have written about 400 words. I email what I've written, which is called a runner, to my editor, who checks it for spelling mistakes and thinks of a headline.

**16:30** I continue writing up the best bits and start to think about the beginning and the ending – the top and the tail – of

the story. At 75 minutes I send what I've done to my editor. With 15 minutes to go, the story is pretty much written. Once I've sent the top and the tail, I cross my fingers that there are no more goals. Fans love it when their team scores a winning goal in the final minutes, but it's stressful as I have to rewrite the top and tail – and only have a few minutes to do it. In fact, the noise of journalists frantically typing is almost as loud as the fans' cheers!

16:45 I finish writing on the final whistle. My story is published online. But I can't go home yet.

17:00 The team coaches go into a room one at a time to answer questions from journalists.

17:30 I quickly rewrite the story to include anything interesting that the coaches said, and also add extra detail I forgot the first time! This is the second version of the story.

17:45 When the players leave the changing rooms for the team bus, they walk through the "mixed zone", a room full of journalists. The players can choose to talk to reporters if they want to. Mixed zones can be very busy. You need good hearing, sturdy legs and sharp elbows to survive! Usually, the comments from players will be used in a separate story the following day. By this time I'm exhausted and it's time to go home.

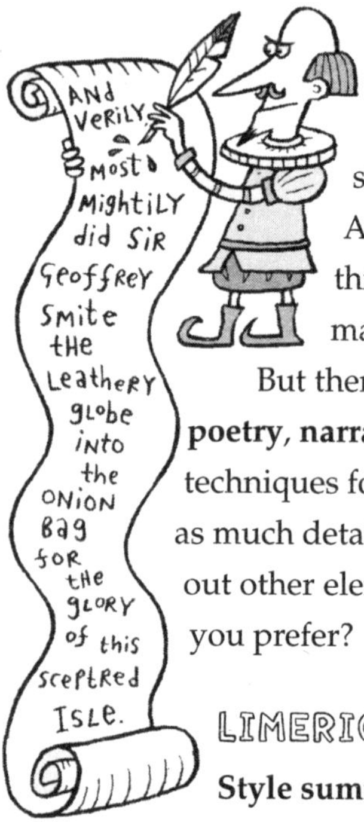


## WRITING WITH STYLE

A match report is the correct writing style for a newspaper or a sports website. As we saw earlier, match reports are in the third person, with simple language and many verbs.

But there are other writing styles, such as **poetry**, **narrative** or **dialogue**, which have their own techniques for telling stories. They may not give you as much detail as a match report, but they can bring out other elements of what happened. Which one do you prefer?

### LIMERICK

**Style summary:** a funny rhyming poem, five lines long.

There once was a striker called Hurst,
Whose World Cup hat-trick was a first;
Each time that he scored
The Wembley fans roared
West Germany left feeling cursed.

### HAIKU

**Style summary:** a poem of seventeen beats, or syllables, in three lines of five, seven and five syllables respectively.

England are world champs
Beat West Germany 4–2
Arise Sir Geoff Hurst

## DIARY

**Style summary:** first person, meaning told from the perspective of one individual who shares their opinions and emotions.

Dear Diary, my name is Geoffrey and I am twenty-four and a half years old. Yesterday I played for England in the World Cup final and scored three goals! We won 4-2 and the whole country celebrated. My mum told me I might become a Sir. That would be so exciting! What I really want is to win the League with my team West Ham and win the World Cup again one day. I wonder if that might happen? If not, I hope I will be remembered in a book called *Football School*!

## DIALOGUE

**Style summary:** a conversation which tells its own story.

**GEOFFREY:** Thanks for that pass, Bobby. It set me up perfectly to score my third goal!

**BOBBY:** You played so well, young Geoffrey. I'm so happy we won the World Cup!

**GEOFFREY:** It's a dream come true. And you, our fantastic England captain, will soon be lifting the World Cup trophy!

## PHONE ME IN

Before computers and emails, journalists used to read out their match reports over the phone to typists in the office. Sometimes a crackly line could lead to embarrassing mistakes. In 1998, one reporter phoned his newspaper to say that England fans were involved in a fight in France during the World Cup. He ended by saying: "A police van drew up containing a dozen armed gendarmes." A *gendarme* is a French policeman. The typist on the other end of the line misheard, and in the next day's paper, it was reported that the police turned up with "a dozen armed John Barnes" – the former Liverpool winger who had recently played for England. But there is only one of him! *Mon dieu*!

# ENGLISH QUIZ

**1. When a reporter sends through their final match report, what have they added at the last minute?**

a) Top and tail
b) Heads and tails
c) Fairy tale
d) Gareth Bale

**2. "Some people are on the pitch! They think it's all over!" What were the next words that BBC commentator Kenneth Wolstenholme used to describe England's fourth goal in the 1966 World Cup final?**

a) "Get off the pitch!"
b) "Come on England!"
c) "It is now!"
d) "Oh Mr Hurst, I think I love you!"

**3. The UK's first newspaper was published in November 1665. What was it called?**

a) *The Times of London*
b) *The Oxford Gazette*
c) *The Newcastle Argus*
d) *Your News Week*

**4. How did the names of former Wales strikers Ian Rush and Mark Hughes supposedly once appear in a match report that was phoned in over a crackly line?**

a) Russian Jews
b) Rushing Poos
c) Rushing Whos
d) Russian News

**5. Which team won the 1999 Champions League final by beating Bayern Munich 2–1 after scoring two goals in the last three minutes of injury-time – forcing journalists to rewrite their match reports in double-quick time?**

a) Chelsea
b) Arsenal
c) Manchester United
d) Liverpool

Wednesday
Lesson 5

# RELIGIOUS STUDIES

What does football teach us? We know that to be a top athlete you have to practise, exercise and eat well; we learn complicated regulations like the offside rule; we discover weird facts such as Everton's nickname being the Toffees.

But there are other things we learn from football too. Things that are nothing to do with football, but are instead about how we live our lives. Deep or what!

Traditionally people have looked to religion for guidance about how to live their lives. There are many religions in the world and they all have similar messages about how to be a good person, such as stating you should not kill or steal.

Today we are going to see how some of the life lessons that religion teaches us can also be found in football.

Hallelujah!

# FAITH ROVERS

A religion is a system of beliefs about the meaning of life. Not everyone belongs to a religion, and that's fine too! Here are five of the world's major religions and how they compare.

| RELIGION | WHEN FOUNDED | HOW MANY FOLLOWERS | KEY FIGURES |
|---|---|---|---|
| Buddhism | More than 2,500 years ago | Around 0.5 billion | Buddha |
| Christianity | 2,000 years ago | Around 2.2 billion | God, Jesus Christ |
| Hinduism | More than 3,000 years ago | Around 0.9 billion | Brahma, Shiva, Vishnu |
| Islam | 1,400 years ago | Around 1.7 billion | Allah, Muhammad |
| Judaism | More than 3,000 years ago | Around 17 million | God, Moses |

| CENTRAL BELIEFS | PLACE OF WORSHIP | FESTIVAL |
|---|---|---|
| The way to free yourself from suffering – nd achieve a state called nirvana – is to follow the teachings of Buddha. Followers learn how to meditate, which is a way to empty your mind of thoughts. | Temple | Vesak, which celebrates Buddha's birthday |
| God sent His Son, Jesus Christ, to Earth in rder to save mankind from the consequences of its own bad behaviour. Jesus was killed on the cross, but came to life again three days later. | Church | Christmas, which celebrates the birth of Jesus Christ |
| Your soul is eternal and when you die it may be born again, or reincarnated, into a different body, such as an animal or a plant. The sacred Hindu texts are called the Vedas. | Temple | Diwali, or the Festival of Lights, celebrates the symbolic victory of light over dark |
| Allah sent his prophet Muhammad to Earth. Through Muhammad, Allah's words were written in the Qur'an, Islam's holy book. | Mosque | Ramadan, which celebrates the month when the verses of the Qur'an were revealed to Muhammad |
| God created the universe, but He has not yet sent His Son to Earth. | Synagogue | Yom Kippur, the day when Jews fast and ask for forgiveness |

## LIFE LESSON 1:
## IT FEELS GOOD TO BELONG

Most human beings love to feel part of something. It is comforting to know that there are other people in the world like us, who share our beliefs and our passions. Traditionally, we get this sense of community from our family, our friends and our religion. Most religions have rituals and festivals that bring people together, like Christmas for Christians and Ramadan for Muslims. In Western Europe, where people are less religious than they used to be, many people now get a sense of belonging in other ways, such as by supporting a football team. When we meet someone who supports the same team as us, we immediately feel a connection with them. When we are in a football stadium surrounded by thousands of fans of the same team, this sense of belonging can be amazing – especially when we are all singing the same song!

| TEAM | PLACE OF WORSHIP | FAVOURITE HYMN |
|---|---|---|
| Bayern Munich | Allianz Arena | "FC Bayern Forever Number One" |
| Juventus | Juventus Stadium | "Storia Di Un Grande Amore" |
| Manchester United | Old Trafford | "Glory Glory Man United" |
| Marseille | Vélodrome | "Allez L'OM!" |
| Real Madrid | Santiago Bernabéu | "Hala Madrid Y Nada Más!" |

## LIFE LESSON 2:
### HAVE A SENSE OF SOMETHING LARGER THAN YOU

Every religion has a belief system that allows its followers to think about their role and position in the universe. It provides us with answers to big questions such as where have we come from and what happens when we die. Religions, in other words, give us a sense of being part of something much bigger than ourselves, which many people find comforting.

 What is a football club? For sure, it is bigger than any single person or thing. A club is made up of the players, the stadium, the fans, the songs, the trophies, the kits, the games and much else besides. A fan's deep love for their club is a way of being devoted to something much larger than they are – something that has existed for decades before they were born, and will continue to exist after they die.

# I'M DYING TO SEE THEM WIN

Some fans are so devoted to their team that they want to be with them even after they die. Several clubs have opened cemeteries for supporters, where gravestones are adorned with club scarves and choirs sing club anthems. Here are some clubs that you can support from beyond the grave:

**Boca Juniors (Argentina)**: Boca's pitch was damaged when families of fans scattered ashes of loved ones on it, so now Boca has its own burial site. It has reserved a plot for its most famous player, Diego Maradona.

**Corinthians (Brazil)**: There is room for the remains of 70,000 fans at the Corinthians Forever Cemetery. The club says the cemetery is: "For those who are fans from the beginning to the end."

**Schalke 04 (Germany)**: The club offers baptism and wedding services, and now has a cemetery for fans. No wonder their team song contains the line "a lifelong blue-and-white".

## LIFE LESSON 3:
## LOSING IS AS IMPORTANT AS WINNING

Religions bring people together for happy celebrations. But religions also have rituals where followers must experience some form of suffering. For example, followers of certain religions must deprive themselves of something during particular religious festivals or holy days. Christians give up habits such as eating chocolate during Lent. Jews, Muslims, Hindus and Buddhists all observe periods of **fasting**, which means they stop eating altogether. The idea behind these rituals is that in order to appreciate how comfortable your life is, you must experience what it is like to be without that comfort. You need to experience suffering to fully experience joy. The message is that sometimes we win and sometimes we lose. Both winning and losing are inevitable facts of life.

We all like it when our team wins, but being a football fan is not just about winning. It is also about losing. Every football fan knows the gut-wrenching, tear-inducing feeling of disappointment when their team loses an important match. Winning and losing are equal parts of the game.

Fans learn to savour the victories. But we also learn how to cope with the defeats. There are good things about losing, even though it might not seem so at the time! Losing often brings out the best in your friendships, as you comfort each other in defeat. It makes you realize that life has ups and downs. The bad times are what make the good times such happy ones.

### GOD SQUAD

These footballers went on to work in the church:

Peter Knowles (Wolverhampton Wanderers)

Phil Mulryne (Manchester United, Norwich, Northern Ireland)

Gavin Peacock (Newcastle, Chelsea, Queens Park Rangers)

Carlos Roa (Racing, Real Mallorca, Argentina)

Taribo West (Inter Milan, Derby, Nigeria)

## LIFE LESSON 4: NEVER GIVE UP HOPE

Religion gives people hope when things get really bad. Many religions encourage prayer, in which you can ask God for help. (Yes, you can ask God to look kindly on your football team too, but there is no proof that it works!) Some religions also offer hope to believers by saying that when we die our souls will go to Heaven, a happy place. Others teach us that life is constantly changing, and that we can always change it for the better.

At Football School we think that whatever religion you believe in – or even if you don't have a religion – you should never give up on your hopes and dreams. And as a football fan, you never give up hope, since there are many times when teams have triumphed against all the odds. Our favourite example is the 2005 Champions League final between Liverpool and AC Milan.

## THE MIRACLE OF ISTANBUL

The half-time score was AC Milan 3, Liverpool 0. The thousands of fans who had travelled from England to watch the match in Istanbul, Turkey, were looking at a humiliating defeat.

A few Liverpool fans left before the second half, but the majority stayed and sang a rousing rendition of the Liverpool anthem, "You'll Never Walk Alone". Inside the dressing-room, the players could hear the song. It lifted their spirits. The coach, Rafael Benitez, changed the tactics for the second half. It worked; in the space of six minutes in that second half, Liverpool scored three goals. Suddenly it was 3—3. The fans kept singing for their team!

The game went to a penalty shoot-out and Jerzy Dudek was the hero; he kept out three penalties, and Liverpool won the match!

The moral of Liverpool's amazing triumph is that no matter how bad things are, the good days may be just around the corner. In Liverpool's case it took only six minutes to turn around what seemed like an impossible situation.

# AGAINST ALL ODDS

Here are some more football miracles:

**Nottingham Forest**
**Title**: European Cup 1979, 1980
Just after their promotion to the top flight in 1978, Forest went on to win the next two European Cups, in 1979 and 1980.

**Hellas Verona**
**Title**: Serie A 1984/85
The little side only lost two games all season, and stunned Italy's big clubs by winning the only title in the club's history.

**Denmark**
**Title**: Euro 1992
Denmark hadn't even qualified for the tournament but were recalled from their holidays after Yugoslavia were banned. Denmark then beat Germany in the final.

**Greece**
**Title**: Euro 2004
No one thought defensive-minded Greece stood a chance but they beat the Czech Republic in the semi-final and Portugal, the favourites and hosts, in the final.

**Leicester City**
**Title**: 2015/16 Premier League
Leicester had only just avoided relegation the previous season but they stunned the richer teams around them by winning the title in dramatic style.

## CHURCH OF MARADONA

One of the best footballers in history even has a religion named after him. The Church of Maradona is an organization that worships Diego Maradona as God. It celebrates two important days in the life of Argentina's most famous player: 30 October, Diego's birthday, and 22 June, the date of his two goals against England in the 1986 World Cup quarter-final. The Church has over 80,000 members and Maradona fans have even got married at his altar. "It's logical," says one of the Church's founders, Hernán Amez. "Football is a religion to Argentinians; every religion has its God and the god of football is Diego."

# RELIGIOUS STUDIES QUIZ

**1. Which is the world's biggest religion?**

a) Christianity
b) Hinduism
c) Islam
d) Jedi

**2. Which Premier League club had two players called "Jesus" in their squad in the 2016/17 season?**

a) Manchester City
b) Liverpool
c) Southampton
d) Chelsea

**3. What is the traditional Buddhist position for meditating?**

a) Curled up in bed
b) Sitting down
c) Standing on one foot
d) Hanging from a tree

**4. What is Liverpool's 2005 Champions League final win over AC Milan known as?**

a) The Wonder of Gerrard
b) The Revelation of Dudek
c) The Marvel of Benitez
d) The Miracle of Istanbul

**5. Argentine goalkeeper Carlos Roa refused to do what for religious reasons when he played for Spanish side Real Mallorca?**

a) Make any saves
b) Cut his hair
c) Play football before sunset on Saturdays
d) Go to church with his team-mates

# DON'T SKIP THIS

Footballers need to be fit, fast, agile and have a great sense of balance. In this After School Club, we will look at one of the best ways to practise these things at the same time, which is … skipping. You thought skipping was easy? Think again. Boxers are well known for incorporating skipping into their training routines, and footballers do it now too. It's a proper work-out without putting too much stress on your joints. Hop to it!

## Skip 1: Double jump

Jump as high as you can and swing the rope fast, so you get the rope under your feet twice while you are in the air.

**GOOD FOR: Increasing pulse rate**
**DIFFICULTY RATING: 1/4**

## Skip 2: Run skips

You need some space, as this involves jogging and then skipping without stopping your running motion.

**GOOD FOR: improving fitness and balance**
**DIFFICULTY RATING: 2/4**

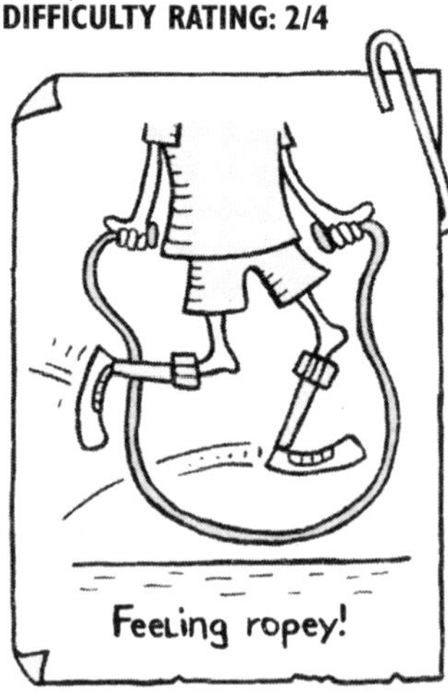

## Skip 3: High Knees

Instead of lifting both feet off the ground at the same time and at the same height, run on the spot and skip; then raise one knee at a time. It's tiring, so only try it for a few swings before going back to normal skipping.

**GOOD FOR: Building leg strength**
**DIFFICULTY RATING: 3/4**

## Skip 4: Crossover

Lift both feet while jumping and swinging the rope normally. Then quickly cross your arms in front of you, stretching your hands as far apart as they can go, and jump through the loop you create. Then cross your hands back so you are skipping normally. It might take some practice to get the loop size right, but it will happen!

**GOOD FOR: Pushing off strongly in sprints**
**DIFFICULTY RATING: 4/4**

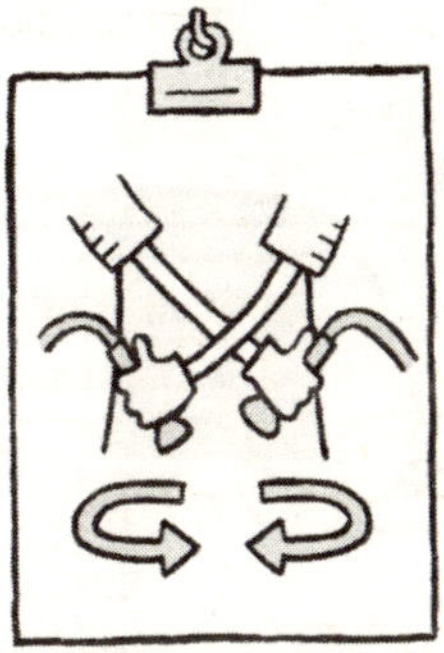

## BEAT IT

The number of times your heart beats every minute is your pulse. When skipping, your pulse should be about 130 beats per minute. To find your pulse, lightly touch the side of your neck until you feel the regular beat. Count how many beats you feel in 10 seconds. Multiply this number by 6 and you have the number of beats per minute.

Thursday
Lesson 1+2

# BIOLOGY

Hands up if you know what **handedness** is! Handedness is the curious way that some people use a pen, press the doorbell or pick their nose with their right hand, while other people prefer their left hand. Nearly all of us use one hand to do most tasks. If we prefer to use the right hand we are right-handed, and if we prefer the left we are left-handed.

We do the same thing with other parts of the body too, such as our eyes and our ears. You might always use your left eye to peer through a keyhole. Or you might always hold your phone to your right ear when you answer it. This is known as **eyedness** and **earedness**.

Let's carry on down to our feet. Most of us prefer to kick a ball with either our left or our right foot. In this lesson we're going to look at **footedness** in football. Are there any advantages to being right-footed or left-footed either on or off the pitch? We're going to investigate the rivalry behind our left and right sides.

Come on, let's get this lesson off on the right foot! Don't get left behind!

# ALL RIGHTIE

First things first: why is there such a thing as handedness anyway? Some scientists say it is because training one hand for a task makes you more skilful at it than if you divided the work between both hands. Being as skilful as possible was very important for survival when we lived in the wild hundreds of thousands of years ago.

For example, imagine two cavemen learning to throw stones. And imagine that one of the cavemen only used his right hand, but the other used his right hand half of the time, and his left hand the other half of the time. The caveman using only his right hand would end up having the best throw, since his right hand would be getting much more practice than either of the hands of the caveman who used both. And if he had the best throw, he would find it easier to throw stones to kill animals for food.

You've probably noticed among your friends that right-handedness is more common. Both Alex and Ben are right-handed.

In fact, so are nine out of every ten people in the world. One amazing aspect of handedness is that it begins from before you are even born. One study found that nine out of ten babies who suck their thumb in the womb do so with their right hand – the same proportion who end up becoming right-handed as adults.

Professor Chris McManus at University College London is a world expert on handedness. He thinks that originally all humans were right-handed. He doesn't know why left-handedness developed, or why there are so many more right-handed people than there are left-handed people. What scientists do know is that half a million years ago there were already some left-handers. They worked this out by looking at fossilized teeth samples. Many of the teeth had scratches at one angle from cutting animal skin with the right hand, but some teeth had scratches at another angle from cutting animal skin with the left hand. Chew, gross!

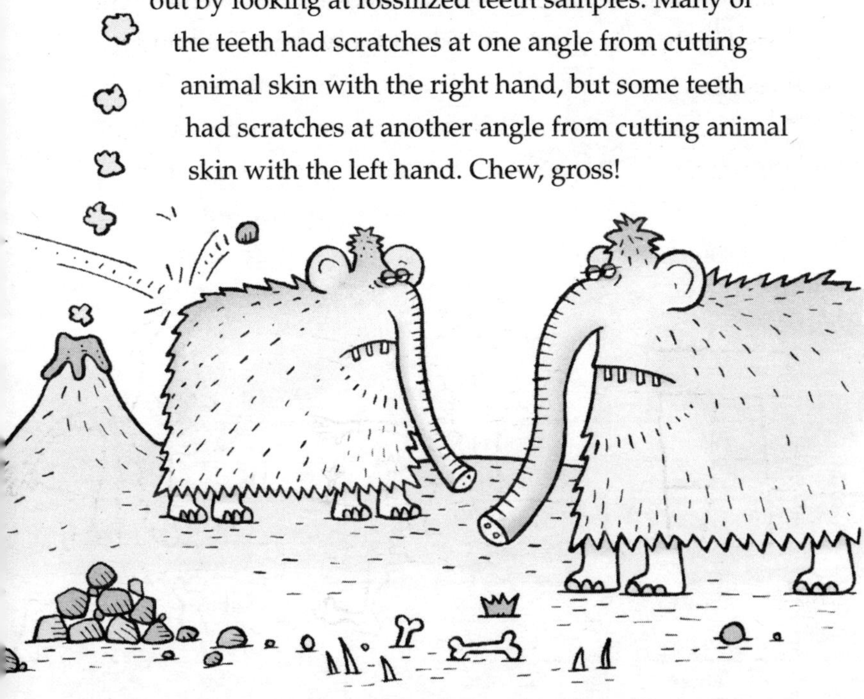

## LEFT ISN'T RIGHT

So, throughout history there have always been fewer lefties than righties, and in many different cultures it seems that lefties have had a worse deal. In ancient Rome, public speakers wore togas that restricted their left side, which meant lefties couldn't make gestures with their good hand. In Europe in the Middle Ages, left-handedness was associated with the devil and witchcraft.

The bad rep for lefties has continued into the modern era. In India, many people eat with their hands, but only the right hand. It is seen as rude to eat with the left hand, because that hand is used for wiping your bum! In Ghana, in Africa, pointing with your left hand is frowned upon.

In many languages the word "right" is associated with good things and the word "left" with bad. In English, "right" means correct. Compare that with the meanings of the word "left" in these languages:

| LANGUAGE | WORD FOR LEFT | OTHER MEANING |
|---|---|---|
| French | Gauche | Clumsy |
| German | Links/Link | Underhand |
| Italian | Sinistra/Sinistro | Sinister |
| Norwegian | Keiv | Wrong |
| Polish | Lewy | Rubbish |
| Portuguese | Canhoto | Devil |
| Turkish | Sol | Odd |

# LET'S SHAKE ON THAT

Even in football, players are encouraged to use their right hands. Before every Premier League game, players shake hands with each other as a gesture of respect. But why do they use their right hands to do this? Some historians think the reason dates back to ancient Greek times, when everyone carried a weapon. If you met someone new, putting out your right hand to show you weren't holding a weapon was a sign of friendship. The up-and-down motion of the handshake was meant to dislodge any knives that might be hidden up a sleeve.

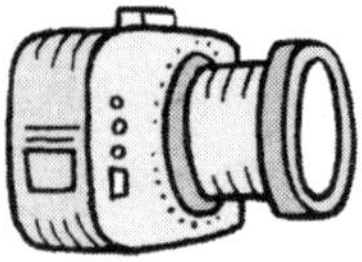

## LEFT BEHIND?

Being left-handed isn't always easy, because many things are designed for people who are right-handed. Here are everyday objects that lefties often struggle with:

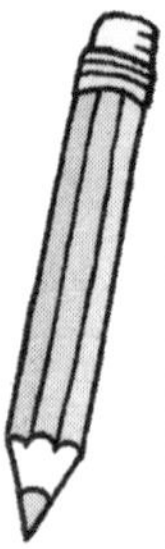

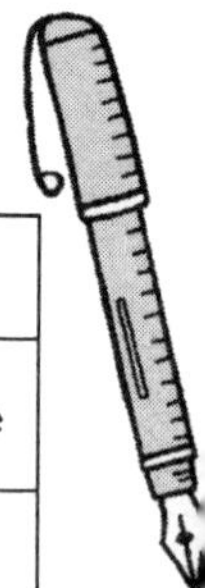

| OBJECT | REASON |
|---|---|
| Camera | Need to use weaker right finger to press shutter |
| Ink pen | Left hand smudges the ink as it moves across the page |
| Pencil sharpener | Difficult to twist a pencil clockwise with your left hand |
| Scissors | Hard to grip right-handed scissors and cut cleanly |
| Zip | Need to use weaker right hand to pull zip |

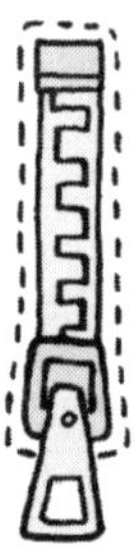

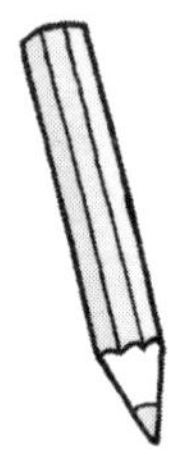

But being left-handed has its advantages too. Surveys have shown that left-handers spend less time in shop queues. This is because people have a tendency to choose the check-out line on their dominant side. So since there are more righties than lefties, queues on the right tend to be busier than queues on the left. And left-handers are more likely on average to pass their UK driving test, which is possibly because they use their dominant (and more skilful) hand on the gear stick.

Professor McManus believes that left-handers' brains are wired in a different way to right-handers', which can sometimes make them more creative people, excelling in music and poetry. Three of the last five American Presidents have been left-handed – many more than you would expect. The same is true of the winners of Nobel Prizes.

However, Professor McManus warns it can work the other way. This same brain-wiring causes some left-handers to have problems with aspects of speech and language.

## LIFE IS SO ONE-SIDED

As you now know, nine out of ten people are right-handed. As a percentage this means that 90 per cent of people are right-handed and 10 per cent are left-handed. The approximate percentages for right dominance and left dominance are different for the other parts of the body:

| BODY PART | RIGHTIES | LEFTIES |
|---|---|---|
| Hand | 90% | 10% |
| Foot | 80% | 20% |
| Eye | 70% | 30% |
| Ear | 60% | 40% |

# LEFT FOOT FORWARD

If you are right-footed, it is more natural to play in a position on the right side of the pitch. This is because your dominant right leg will be nearest the touchline, meaning you are able to use the full width of the pitch. Likewise, if you are left-footed, it is more natural to play on the left.

You might have thought that the tendency for righties to be on the right and lefties to be on the left means that you get more or less the same number of lefties and righties in a team. Surprisingly, however, this is not the case. Dr David Carey of Bangor University found that approximately 80 per cent of professional footballers are right-footed and 20 per cent left-footed, which is the same percentage as for the population as a whole. Dr Carey based his figures on some matches from two World Cups and one full Premier League season.

The fact that the majority of players in any team are right-footed means that often right-footers play on the left. When they play on their "wrong" side, they need to adjust their body shape in order to make the most of that position.

Some of football's best ever players were left-footed. Here are our five greatest players of all time (but not in order). Four are left-footed!

**FIVE GREATEST PLAYERS**

Johan Cruyff (The Netherlands): Leftie
Diego Maradona (Argentina): Leftie
Lionel Messi (Argentina): Leftie
Pelé (Brazil): Rightie
Ferenc Puskás (Hungary): Leftie

Our list is a small sample size, but that number is way higher than the 20 per cent average in football. Maybe it's because right-footers find it harder to play against left-footers because they are rarer – or that lefties are more successful because they are used to finding solutions in a right-handed world!

In some sports, being left-handed can definitely be an advantage. The percentage of successful left-handed professionals in cricket, tennis, baseball, fencing and boxing – where left-handers are known as "southpaws" – is also much higher than average. Experts think it's because being left-handed adds an element of surprise to their game, as right-handers have less experience playing against lefties.

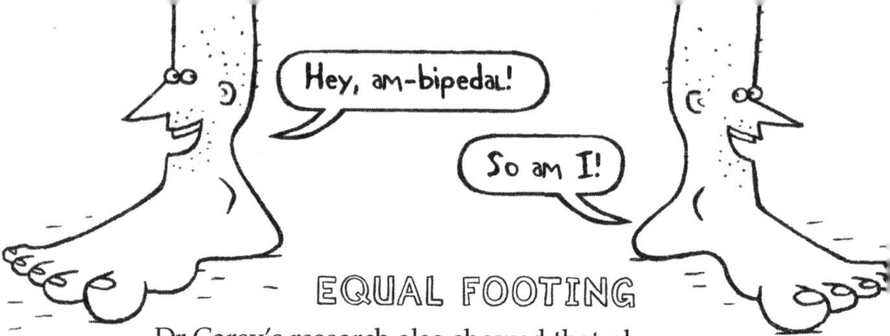


## EQUAL FOOTING

Dr Carey's research also showed that players use their dominant foot 80 per cent of the time on the pitch – but that they are actually more successful with their passes when using their other, weaker, foot. He thinks that this is because players only use their weaker foot in easy situations, and make risky passes with the dominant foot.

Some people can be equally good with both their left or right sides. Those who are equally good with their right and left hands are called **ambidextrous** from the Latin for "ambi", meaning "both", and "dexter" meaning "right side".

The foot equivalent of ambidextrous is **ambipedal**, although if a footballer is just as good with either foot we say they are **two-footed** – even though all professional footballers have two feet! Dr Carey calculated that only 1 in 1,000 male players are truly two-footed.

Spanish midfielder Santi Cazorla is two-footed. He once injured his right foot (his dominant one) and then practised with his left so much that now he can take corners with either foot – and he doesn't even know which is better! And it turns out that Cazorla was on to something: another study of over 3,000 players showed that left-footed players earn a little more money than their right-footed colleagues. But those who are two-footed can earn up to 15 per cent more than right-footed players.

## RIGHT GIRLS

We said that 90 per cent of the population is right-handed and 10 per cent is left-handed. If we separate those numbers into men and women, we see that 12 per cent of men are lefties, but only 9 per cent of women. No one knows why more men are left-handed, but it could be because girls born left-handed are more likely to switch handedness at an early age than boys.

This also applies on the pitch. Dr Carey looked at all the women who played in the 2011 World Cup finals and the 2012 Olympics. He compared this to his data on male footballers and discovered that women footballers on average are less likely to be left-footed:

| FOOT | FOOTBALLERS (FEMALE) | FOOTBALLERS (MALE) |
|---|---|---|
| Right-footed | 87.5% | 79.8% |
| Left-footed | 11.1% | 20.1% |
| Two-footed | 1.3% | 0.1% |

## CROSSED PLAYERS

Some players have their handedness and footedness all mixed up! These footballers are right-handed but left-footed:

# BIOLOGY QUIZ

**1. What do you call a left-handed boxer?**

a) Northpaw
b) Eastpaw
c) Westpaw
d) Southpaw

**2. In what sport is it illegal to play left-handed?**

a) Golf
b) Polo
c) Badminton
d) Tiddlywinks

**3. Which animal is almost exclusively left-handed?**

a) Meerkat
b) Frog
c) Kangaroo
d) Baboon

**4. Paolo Maldini played over 900 games for AC Milan and won seven Italian league titles and five Champions League titles with them. He was two-footed. Which of the following is true?**

a) One of his feet was two sizes bigger than the other
b) He spent his whole career playing as a left-back
c) He was scared to shoot with his right foot
d) The only goals he ever scored were with his head

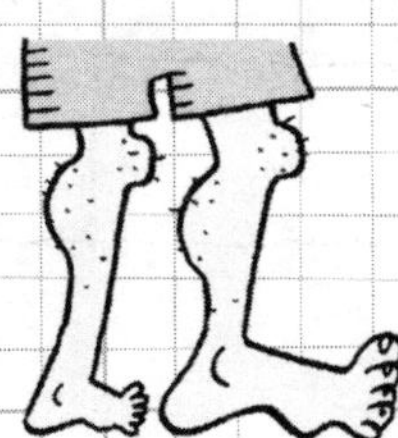

**5. What are the chances of one identical twin being left-handed and the other right-handed?**

a) 0 per cent
b) 20 per cent
c) 50 per cent
d) 100 per cent

Thursday
Lesson 3+4

# MATHS

Football is about numbers. It's a game of 11 versus 11, for 90 minutes, in which each team tries to score a greater number of goals than their opponent. League tables are grids of digits: wins, draws, losses, matches played, goal difference and total points. All these numbers are why Alex loves it!

But that's just the start. Football is full of **data** and **statistics** (or **stats**), which are facts that can be described with numbers. Before a match, you will hear commentators give team stats such as how many times the teams have played each other before and which team won the most times. After a game there will be data to show how long each team had possession of the ball, how many shots on goal there were and many other facts. A data deluge! A swamp of statistics!

In this lesson we are going to find out how football data is collected and then look at how it can be used to give us fascinating insights into the game.

Let the countdown begin!

# SPEED DATA

At the beginning of every Premier League match, in an office far away from the stadium, two people will be sitting in front of a bank of computer screens, ready to turn that match into numbers.

As soon as the whistle is blown, these **data gatherers** start typing away on their keyboards. Tap, tap, tap, tap! The moment a player touches the ball, they type in his shirt number and also what he does with the ball, such as "pass" or "cross", from a list of many actions. There are two data gatherers because getting all that information is too much for just one person to do. They split the load – one types in the data for the home team and the other for the away team.

The data gatherers must stay focused for the entire match so that every detail is captured. No sneezing or scratching your bum! As well as "pass" and "cross", there are about 50 different events they need to type in if they see it happening on the pitch. Some are obvious and easy to register, such as "goal", "corner" and "red card". But there are others that require eagle-eyes and good judgement, such as "flick on", "good skill" and "interception". One of the screens has an aerial diagram of the pitch, on which they click the position of the ball each time it is kicked.

At the end of the game, the gatherers quickly check for mistakes and then send all the data to companies like TV channels and newspapers. Then they can finally relax. It's been an exhausting 90 minutes for their eyes, fingers and brains.

## GATHERING GIFTS

Gathering football data is done by humans rather than by computer since computers are not good enough (yet!) to do the job properly. For example, when a dozen players jump together for a ball from a corner, a human data gatherer is able to judge who headed the ball by looking at details like the players' facial expressions, hairstyles and maybe even the colour of their shoes. Computers don't have a clue!

Being a data gatherer sounds like a fun job, since all you do is watch football matches. But not every human has the required skills. You need to have very good **hand-eye coordination**, which means that you can move your hands based on what you see very quickly and accurately. Gatherers know exactly where to move their hands on the keyboard without ever looking down.

Most people who apply to be gatherers don't have the necessary technical skills to do the job. Even those who do spend four to six weeks training on demo games for eight hours a day. After the training it still takes several months to become confident. During any one game, the gatherers will register about 2,000 pieces of data, which works out as one piece of data about every two seconds. That's what you call being on the ball!

## STATS R US

We collect all this data in order to understand the game better. Numbers allow us to discover football facts that we would not otherwise know. If we look at data from the history of English football's top flight (meaning the First Division from 1888–1992, and the Premier League from 1992–2017) then it is easy to find out some very intriguing stats:

## NUMBERS GAME

**7 goals** were scored by Ted Drake for Arsenal against Aston Villa in December 1935, which remains the most goals ever scored by a player in a single game in the top league of English football.

**0–0** is the most common scoreline in the Premier League.

**89 minutes** is the most likely minute of the game in regular time for a goal to be scored (excluding goals scored on 45 minutes and 90 minutes, because these take into account injury time).

**168 passes** were made by Yaya Touré when playing for Manchester City against Stoke City in December 2011, which is the most passes any Premier League player has made since this data was first gathered in 2006.

# PERFECT PERCENTAGES

Sometimes we need to do some maths to make the statistics easier to understand. Today we're going to learn about **percentages** and **averages**.

Percentages are a way to describe amounts as a proportion of one hundred, and are used as a way to make different numbers easy to compare. For example, this diagram shows where on the pitch all Premier League goals from 1992–2017 have been scored from:

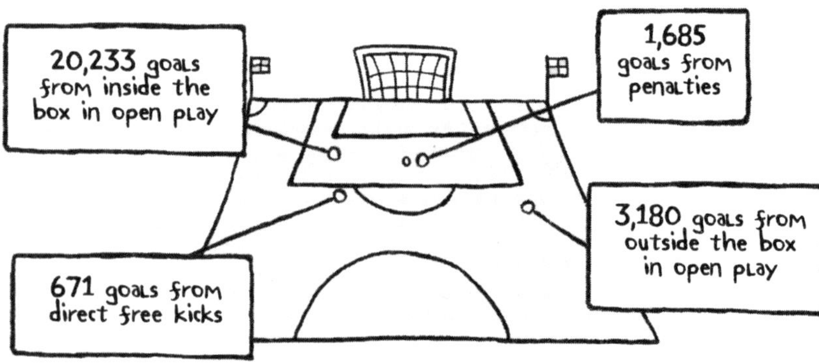


That's a lot of goals! But it is not very clear how the numbers relate to each other. It's much easier if we turn them into percentages:

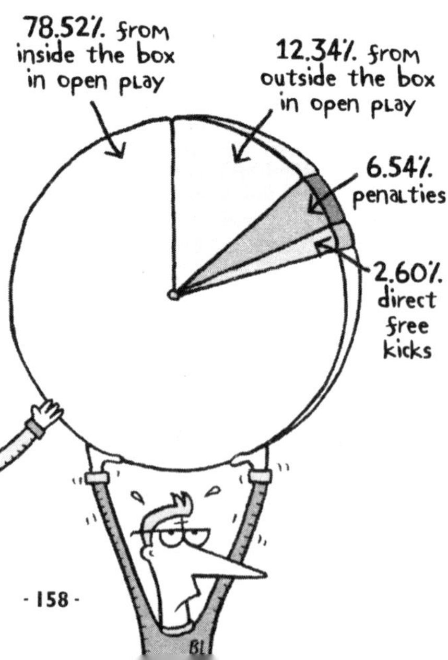

The numbers in the pie chart mean that out of every 100 goals, about 79 came from inside the box in open play, about 12 came from outside the box in open play, about 7 came from penalties and about 3 came from direct free kicks (rounding to the nearest number). One hundred is a nice easy number to make comparisons from, which is why percentages make things easier to understand.

### PERCENTAGE PROBLEM

Since Ben loves penalties, we'll show him here how to calculate the percentage of goals scored by penalties. First, we need to count the total number of goals of all kinds, which adds up to **25,769**. Then we divide the number of goals scored from penalties by the total, like this:

1,685 ÷ 25,769 = 0.0654

Then we multiply this by **100**:

0.0654 x 100 = 6.54%

There we have it! **6.54%** of goals are scored from penalties. The way of calculating percentages is always the same: divide the number of particular events (e.g. how a goal is scored) by the number of total events (e.g. all goals scored) and then multiply by **100**.

Sometimes football coaches say that their team "gave 110 per cent", which means that football coaches are very bad at maths! No one can give more than 100 per cent, since 100 per cent of something means ALL of that thing. To say that the team gave 110 per cent is an exaggeration that means the team gave everything they could give – and more. At Football School, we mock these coaches for not exaggerating enough. Here we insist on 111 per cent!

# AWESOME AVERAGES

Sometimes matches have no goals (boo!) and sometimes matches have lots of goals (yay!). We can use maths to work out how many goals there are **on average** per game.

This statistic does not mean that in every match 2.64 goals are scored – that would be impossible! What it means is that sometimes there are fewer than 2.64 goals and sometimes there are more than 2.64 goals, but if we take all Premier League games from 1992–2017 together, then a good estimate for the typical number of goals is 2.64. This is the **average** number.

## AVERAGE SUM

We calculate the average number of goals per match by adding up all the goals scored in all games and dividing them by the total number of games:

25,769 ÷ 9,746= 2.64

The average number of goals per Premier League game between 2010 and 2017 is 2.75, a little bit higher than the average of all games between 1992 and 2017. Compare these figures to the averages in different leagues. In Germany you will see, on average, almost half a goal more per game than in France.

| AUG 2010–17 | AVERAGE NUMBER OF GOALS PER GAME |
|---|---|
| German Bundesliga | 2.90 |
| Spanish La Liga | 2.78 |
| English Premier League | 2.75 |
| Italian Serie A | 2.67 |
| French Ligue 1 | 2.50 |

# HOME RULES

Most football fans know that there is an advantage to playing at home, since teams tend to perform better in their own stadiums. There are many reasons why this is true, such as familiarity with the stadium, being surrounded by all your supporters and not having to travel very far to get to the match. What's great about maths is that we can use it to work out exactly how much better teams do at home than away.

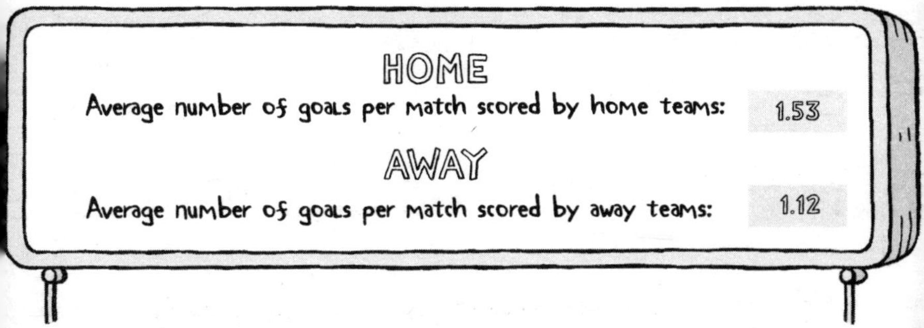


If teams score, on average, 1.53 goals per game at home but only 1.12 goals away, then, on average, teams are scoring 1.53 – 1.12 = 0.41 more goals when playing at home than when playing away. The home advantage is almost half a goal per match!

# ON TARGET

The shot conversion rate is the number of times a shot at goal will result in a goal. The percentage is calculated by dividing the number of shots that score goals by the number of all shots at goal. Here are the top ten best teams from 2010–17. The average shot conversion rate across all clubs is 12.91 per cent, which shows how good the best ones are!

| CLUB | SHOT CONVERSION RATE (%) |
|---|---|
| Barcelona | 22.24 |
| Real Madrid | 19.38 |
| RB Leipzig | 19.08 |
| Bayern Munich | 18.52 |
| Paris Saint-Germain | 17.82 |
| Manchester City | 16.89 |
| Manchester United | 16.85 |
| Monaco | 16.69 |
| Borussia Dortmund | 16.62 |
| Arsenal | 16.38 |

# MATHS QUIZ

**1. What does "stats" stand for?**

a) Statues
b) Statistics
c) Stalactites
d) Stationary

**2. Which of these jobs requires the best hand-eye coordination?**

a) Librarian
b) Teacher
c) Model
d) Bus driver

**3. What is 50 per cent of 90 minutes?**

a) 45 minutes
b) 50 minutes
c) 90 minutes
d) 110 minutes

**4. If a team plays four games and scores the following number of goals – 1, 1, 2, 4 – in the games, what is the average number of goals the team scores per game?**

a) 1
b) 2
c) 3
d) 4

**5. What does the common phrase "big data" mean?**

a) Data about fat people
b) A species of large dates grown in Cyprus
c) Lots and lots of data
d) DATA written in capital letters

Thursday
Lesson 5

# PSYCHOLOGY

Being a football coach is just like being a teacher. Both coaches and teachers want their players, or pupils, to learn, develop, be happy and perform as well as they can. They also want them to be quiet when they're talking, not make too much mess and not pull faces behind their backs!

You'll know that teachers can be very different. Some are very strict, some love bad jokes. Some explain everything and some leave you to work things out.

And pupils are very different too. Some pupils do their homework as soon as possible, while others leave it to the last minute. Some pupils hate to speak in class, while others love the sound of their own voice.

The same is true in football. There are many coaching styles, and each player is different. The challenge for a coach is to find a style of leadership that gets the best out of each individual player and gets the whole team to improve. In order to do that, the coach needs to understand what makes each player respond: will the threat of punishment or an arm around the shoulder work best?

Coaches aren't just the people in charge of tactics. They are also **psychologists**, which is what we call people who are experts in how the human mind works.

Now, are you still listening at the back?

## WHAT TYPE OF COACH ARE YA?

There are lots of different ways to lead a team. Look at these four famous coaches and see if any remind you of your favourite – or your least favourite – teacher!

### 1. THE HUGGER: JÜRGEN KLOPP

***Teams coached**: Mainz 05, Borussia Dortmund, Liverpool*

The mood at the Liverpool Christmas party in 2016 was low. Earlier in the day, the team had lost to Watford. But coach Jürgen Klopp did not want the players to be sad. He told everyone to forget about the game, have fun and do a lot of dancing. He jumped onto the dancefloor and made everyone laugh. This is one of the ways that Klopp gets the best out of his teams. His use of humour makes people like him – and if you like someone, you are likely to work hard for them!

Klopp spends 70 per cent of his time keeping everyone happy. He believes that TEAM stands for: Together Everyone Achieves More. Klopp is often laughing on the touchline. He also hugs his players a lot to show that he cares about them. Scientific studies have shown that team-mates who hug or touch each other a lot are more likely to be successful. Even if his team has lost, Klopp's players will still get a hug. "The emotion makes the difference," he says. Kloppo cares!

## 2. THE DEEP THINKER: PEP GUARDIOLA

***Teams coached:*** *Barcelona, Bayern Munich, Manchester City*

All coaches want to beat their opponents. Pep Guardiola spends hours watching videos to work out weaknesses in other teams. Friends say he can only switch off for 32 minutes before he starts thinking about football again!

Guardiola is not afraid to come up with new solutions to win matches. He famously switched Lionel Messi's position at Barcelona to help make him one of the world's best players. In the same team, Zlatan Ibrahimović was sold because he did not fit in with Pep's ideas. Guardiola regularly puts full-backs in midfield or even midfielders in defence if he feels it will help the team use the ball better.

OTHER THINKERS:
Marcelo Bielsa
Mauricio Pochettino
Jorge Sampaoli
Thomas Tuchel

His players call him a perfectionist. He believes that football should be played in a certain way: by keeping possession of the ball for as long as possible before creating chances. If the players are willing to learn, he is a teacher who will challenge them to the limit and lead them to great victories.

## 3. THE QUIET LEADER: CARLO ANCELOTTI

***Teams coached:*** *Reggiana, Parma, Juventus, AC Milan, Chelsea, Paris Saint-Germain, Real Madrid, Bayern Munich*

Carlo Ancelotti is known for being naturally quiet and open-minded. He will often change his ideas to find the right solution. He's coached some of the biggest clubs in the world and is liked wherever he goes. That's impressive!

It helps that Ancelotti speaks lots of languages. He was also a successful player, winning three Italian league titles and two European Cups. He played in midfield, where he was known for quietly making things happen.

He is similar as a coach: he can fit into any club environment and get results. The loudest person in the room is not always the best; Ancelotti speaks quietly and rarely, but when he does, it's worth listening. Often Ancelotti lets players decide on the strategy they want to use for games.

He does not have a preferred style of football. When he was coach at Juventus, he changed the team's system to accommodate the great French midfielder Zinedine Zidane. At Real Madrid, he moved things around to get the best out of forward Cristiano Ronaldo. The skill of the quiet leader is to look like you are not doing too much, when actually you are.

# 4. THE TEACHER: ARSÈNE WENGER

***Teams coached**: Nancy, Monaco, Nagoya Grampus Eight, Arsenal*

One newspaper ran the headline "Arsène Who?" when Arsenal appointed Arsène Wenger as coach in 1996. Everyone soon knew exactly who he was. The Frenchman quickly won three Premier League titles, including the 2003/04 season when the team did not lose a single game. Invincible!

Wenger's success at Arsenal changed many things in football. Teams followed his approach to nutrition: he banned sweets, chocolate and fizzy drinks from the training-ground. He also introduced regular stretching sessions for his players before training. Some of his older players said this allowed them to play on for an extra few years. Other teams became less nervous about appointing foreign coaches, or signing foreign players.

Wenger's key principle was to pick young players and help them improve. He was not afraid to select even very young players. "He is a teacher first, a manager second, a tactician third," said one Arsenal fan who knows him. Wenger said of his own influence: "I felt like I was opening the door to the rest of the world."

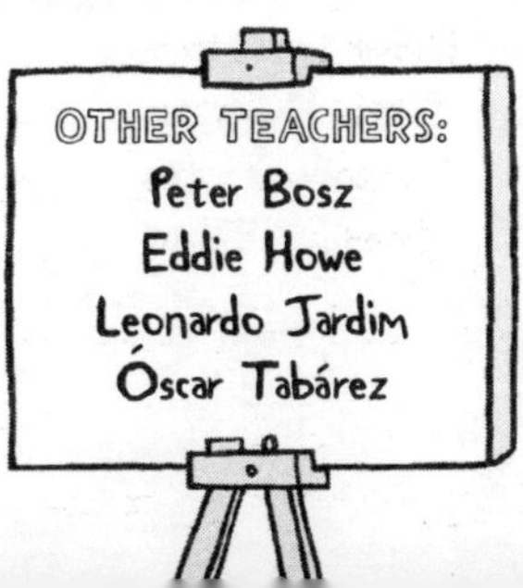

## THE NAME'S BONDING ... TEAM BONDING

A good coach is always looking for ways to help the team bond. After all, if you understand and like your team-mates, you may try that bit harder to help them on the pitch. Here are some wacky methods that coaches have tried:

### SHEEP-HERDING

When he was Burnley coach, Eddie Howe wanted his players to raise the baa (geddit?!), so he took them on a surprise trip to a farm in Bristol. They were split into two groups and each group had to round up ten sheep and herd them into a pen in the middle of a field. At the time, he thought it was a good exercise in leadership and teamwork. He later admitted that he got annoyed with some of the players. "It was a moment, for me, of understanding that with the modern footballer there are some things you can't do," Howe said. "Sheep-herding might be one of them."

## SWAN LAKE

Graham Potter has been the most successful coach in the history of Östersunds FK, a small club based in Sweden. Since Potter joined the club in 2011, ÖFK have gone from the fourth division to the first division – thanks to some rather unique managerial methods. Every year, Potter asks his players to work together on a cultural project. One year they collaborated to write a book. In 2016, they performed a modern dance version of the 1877 ballet *Swan Lake*. "If you want to develop them as people, you have to have those uncomfortable experiences," Potter said. "As a team, if we all understand that, then we can help each other."

## PIZZA-FLIPPING

Coach Claudio Ranieri rewarded his Leicester City players for not conceding a goal in a game against Crystal Palace by taking them out for a pizza-making lesson. The whole squad joined in, flipping dough and adding their own toppings. "It's the team spirit and they enjoy training," said Italian boss Ranieri. "A little bit of luck is important. Luck is the salt, the fans are the tomato – with no tomato there is no pizza." It did the trick: Leicester went on to win the Premier League. *Bravissimo*, Claudio!

## BINGO!

Leeds United were English champions twice under coach Don Revie, back in 1969 and 1974. The former Leeds player immediately fostered a united spirit in the squad. He organized social nights for the players and their families, which included playing dominoes and bingo. "Our whole ethos was built on loyalty," said midfielder Peter Lorimer. "We all fight for each other, we all work for each other." That's true teamwork. (Or as they say in bingo, Duck and Dive – Twenty-Five!)

# THE CLOCK IS TICKING

Being a football coach is a powerful job – but it could be over very quickly. You are responsible for the team results, which might affect the size of the TV broadcast and club sponsorship deals. You also need to keep everyone fully motivated and ready to give their all – not just the eleven players who start each game, but the others who are not picked. It's important that the fans and owners like you too. Here are some coach appointments that didn't work out so well:

**Coach**: Leroy Rosenior
**How long in the job**: 10 minutes
**Club/Year**: Torquay, 2007
**Reason**: A new owner came in just after his appointment and sacked him.

**Coach**: Marcelo Bielsa
**How long in the job:** 2 days
**Club/Year**: Lazio, 2016
**Reason**: The players he was promised would be bought were not and so he left.

**Coach**: Dave Bassett
**How long in the job**: 4 days
**Club/Year**: Crystal Palace, 1984
**Reason**: Bassett realized he preferred his old club Wimbledon, so went back there.

# FERGIE'S LIFE LESSONS

Sir Alex Ferguson was Manchester United's most successful coach ever. He once discussed his top management tips, which we list here. At Football School we think these are great ideas to follow.

1. Start with the foundation
2. Dare to rebuild
3. Set high standards
4. Never give up control
5. Match the message to the moment
6. Prepare to win
7. Rely on the power of observation
8. Never stop adapting

# PSYCHOLOGY QUIZ

**1. What is a psychologist?**

a) Someone who is an expert in the human mind and human behaviour
b) Someone who can tell the future
c) Someone who can score three goals in every game
d) An expert in dancing to the Psy song "Gangnam Style"

**2. What is a perfectionist?**

a) Someone who is perfect
b) Someone who loves perfect people
c) Someone who only accepts perfection
d) Someone who purrs

**3. How many people took part in the largest group hug in the world, recorded in Canada in 2010?**

a) 1,055
b) 10,554
c) 105,554
d) 1,554,000

**4. Which of the following coaches is a Hugger?**

a) Zinedine Zidane
b) Antonio Conte
c) Eddie Howe
d) Thomas Tuchel

**5. Why did Arsène Wenger ban fizzy drinks from the training-ground?**

a) The players kept burping during matches
b) Too much sugar was bad for the players
c) The floor was always sticky because they spilt the drinks
d) The players were weeing too much

HEALTH
AFTER SCHOOL CLUB

# SMOOTHIE BAR

What footballers eat and drink is not only important on match day, but all season long. Players try to eat the healthiest foods to keep their fitness up and performance levels high. In this After School Club, we'll show you how easy it is to make a healthy snack at home. Just throwing some fruit and veg into a blender can have amazing results! Here are some easy smoothie recipes that everyone at Football School loves. Fruity fun!

## Smoothie 1: Ben's Banana Bonanza

Bananas are packed with nutrients that are brilliant for your body: potassium, which is good for your heart, carbohydrates to give you energy and fibre to improve your digestion. The nuts contain protein which builds cells and muscles in your body.

***Ingredients:*** *1 banana, a handful of walnuts, 2 cups milk, 1 tbsp honey*

***Could also add:*** *Peanut butter, pineapple, cocoa powder, blueberries, ginger*

---

**GOOD FOR: Boosting energy before training**

**TASTE SENSATION: 1/3**

## Smoothie 2: Spike's C-Blaster

This refreshing smoothie made from fruits high in Vitamin C will protect your body in winter and help you recover after training. Vitamin C boosts our immune system and helps us fight off colds and other illnesses. You don't want to have the sniffles when you're through on goal with just the keeper to beat!

***Ingredients:*** *1 grapefruit (peeled), 1 cup pineapple chunks, 1 cup strawberries, ½ cup yoghurt*

***Could also add:*** *mango, orange, kiwi, raspberries, kale*

---

**GOOD FOR: Recovery after training and fighting off illness**
**TASTE SENSATION: 2/3**

## Smoothie 3: Alex's 'Ave-A-Go Avocado

Some scientists claim that certain fruits, such as blueberries and avocados, are really good for the brain. They're certainly delicious, whatever effect they have. Alex loves both blueberries and avocados so maybe that's why he's good at maths!

***Ingredients:*** *½ avocado (peeled), 1 cup blueberries, 1 cup yoghurt, ½ cup milk, juice from ½ lime*

***Could also add:*** *blackcurrant, apple, beetroot, lemon*

---

**GOOD FOR: Overall wellbeing**
**TASTE SENSATION: 3/3**

**FOOD NOTE!** Always ask an adult to help you chop the fruit and use a blender. If you are diabetic or have food allergies ask an adult first.

Friday
Lesson 1–4
ART
I've got you a present!
Oh wow, thanks!
It's something full of prestige ... will make you respected ... will last generations ... will be your legacy...
Sounds brilliant – what is it?
A coat of ARMS!
BL
AB
AB

Every football club has a symbol.

This symbol – called a badge, crest or logo – appears on the team's shirts. It has a practical use: to identify members of that team. But it has another use too. The shapes, colours and words on the badge reflect the club's history and its values. It's as if everything about the club is captured in the badge, which is one reason why many players like to kiss it when they score a goal.

The Football School badge has two 18-yard-boxes, a football, a book and a gold star. These are things that we think say a lot about Football School – that it's a place for fun, for football, for learning and for stars!

Many club badges are inspired by **coats of arms**, which were symbols historically used by armies, rich families, towns and businesses. In this lesson you are going to learn how to create a coat of arms. This coat of arms will tell the story of who you are. And if you ever have your own football team, it can be your team badge too.

Let's get our coats!

## A STITCH IN TIME

Before we start designing our coat of arms, let's take a closer look at what they are and where they came from.

In 1066 the English army was defeated at the Battle of Hastings by an invading force of Normans led by William the Conqueror. Back then there were no cameras. So to remember the victory, a piece of cloth, 70 metres long, was embroidered to show different scenes from the battle, such as the moment the English king Harold was supposedly killed by an arrow to the eye. Eek! This giant piece of cloth is now known as the Bayeux Tapestry.

The tapestry gives us a rare glimpse of what soldiers wore in those days and what equipment they used. And it shows us that some of the soldiers used shields decorated with specific, recognizable images. For example, on some shields was a cross, and on some was an animal. Historians think the armies put these symbols on the shields so the soldiers could quickly see who was a friend and who was an enemy – quite a useful thing to be sure of when you are in the middle of fighting! There was no point writing words on the shields since few soldiers could read.

These military symbols later became known as coats of arms because they were displayed on the tunics worn over armour. The system of rules for the design and use of coats of arms is called **heraldry**.

## HARK THE HERALDRY

A couple of hundred years after the Battle of Hastings, rich and powerful individuals began to copy soldiers and use coats of arms as symbols for their own families. And later, towns and counties got in on the act too, using coats of arms as their symbols.

Then it was football's turn to get involved. In 1875 Blackburn Rovers were the first team in England to wear a symbol on their kit. The team had a Maltese cross, seen on the flag on the left, on the left breast of their shirts. The cross is a symbol associated with knights and each of its eight points symbolizes a specific character trait: truth, faith, repentance, humility, justice, mercy, sincerity and bravery. That was a lot for the Rovers players to think about!

Other clubs adopted their local council's coat of arms. In 1877 Notts County, for example, started wearing a badge with three crowns and a ragged cross on their kits – the City of Nottingham's crest. This may have been because Notts County's line-up was made up of Nottingham's upper class, many of whom played in school rugby teams that sported similar symbols on their shirts.

# CLASH OF SYMBOLS

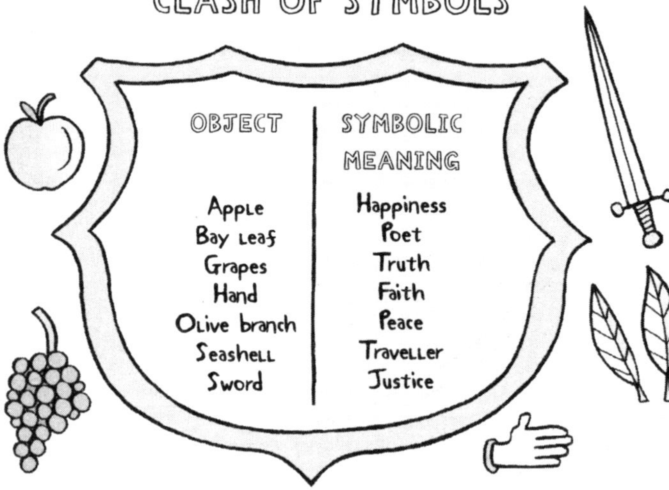

| OBJECT | SYMBOLIC MEANING |
|---|---|
| Apple | Happiness |
| Bay leaf | Poet |
| Grapes | Truth |
| Hand | Faith |
| Olive branch | Peace |
| Seashell | Traveller |
| Sword | Justice |

A coat of arms has several distinctive parts. It normally has a **shield**, two animals that support the shield, known as **shield supporters**, and a short piece of text called a **motto**. The shield can be in any shape or colour you like and be decorated with different objects. The animals can also be anything you fancy – even mythological creatures.

Traditionally, however, the objects, colours and creatures on a coat of arms were understood to be symbols that

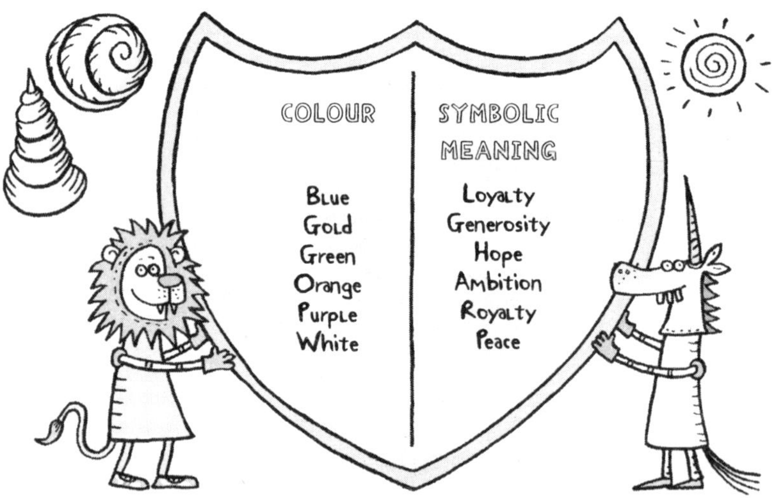

| COLOUR | SYMBOLIC MEANING |
|---|---|
| Blue | Loyalty |
| Gold | Generosity |
| Green | Hope |
| Orange | Ambition |
| Purple | Royalty |
| White | Peace |

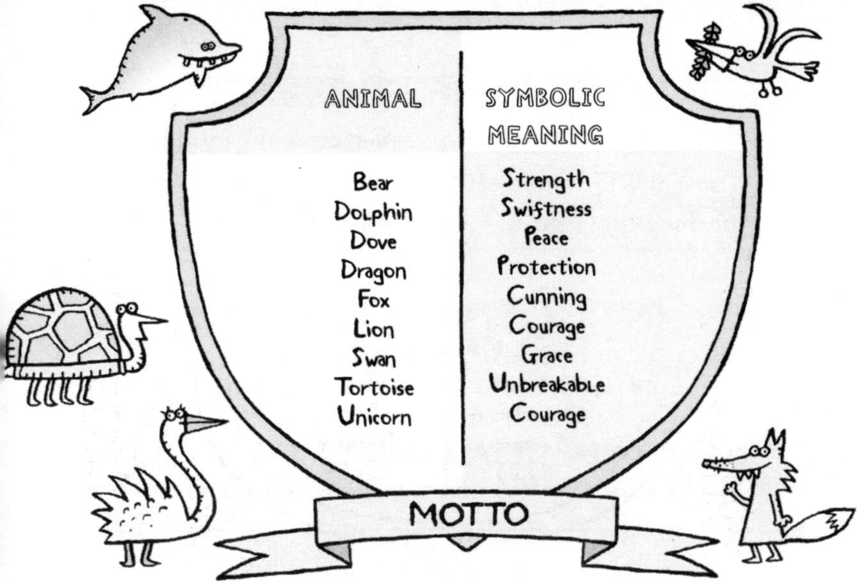


represented something else. For example, an apple meant happiness, a lion meant courage and blue meant loyalty. Using symbols on your coat of arms was a way to show people the skills and attributes you valued, and the kind of person you were.

On this page are some of the meanings of things found on coats of arms. Below are some objects and symbols we invented for today:

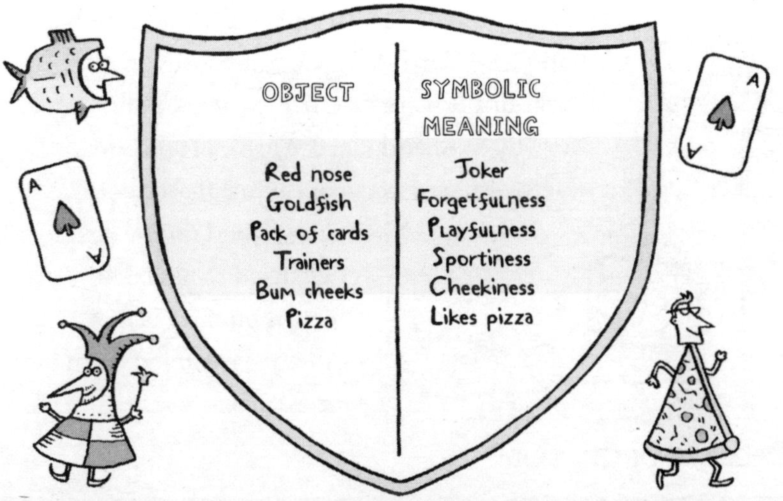

## WHAT A MOTTO LOTTO!

Another important part of a coat of arms is the motto. A motto is a short phrase that sums up your beliefs or way of approaching life. Here are Alex's and Ben's:

> ALEX:
> FAMILIA + NUMERI X ROTAE
> = GAUDIUM
> (Family + maths x wheels = happiness)
>
> BEN: FAMILIA, RISUS ET PIZZA
> (Family together, with laughter and pizza)

Mottos can be in any language you like, but many people choose Latin, the language of ancient Rome that no one speaks any more. Professor Mary Beard of the University of Cambridge says that Latin is perfect for mottos because it can make things snappier and shorter and sound cleverer than in English. Professor Beard says her department is always getting requests from charities and sports clubs to translate English phrases into Latin.

Some football clubs still have Latin mottos on their badge. Bury has *Vincit Omnia Industria*, which is Latin for "Hard Work Conquers All", while Blackburn Rovers has *Arte et Labore*, Latin for "By Skill and Hard Work". (There are a few different ways of saying "hard work" in Latin!) Other clubs, listed on the next page, used to have Latin mottos on their badges but have removed them in recent years:

*BEWARE OF THE DOG

| CLUB | LATIN MOTTO | TRANSLATION |
|---|---|---|
| Arsenal | Victoria Concordia Crescit | Victory Through Harmony |
| Everton | Nil Satis Nisi Optimum | Nothing But the Best is Good Enough |
| Manchester City | Superbia in Proelio | Pride in Battle |
| Sheffield Wednesday | Consilio et Animis | By Wisdom and Courage |
| Tottenham Hotspur | Audere est Facere | To Dare is to Do |

## MARVELLOUS MOTTOS

Here are some of our favourite club mottos:

**Club:** Asante Kotoko (Ghana)
**Motto:** *Kum Apem A, Apem Beba* (Asante Twi)
**Meaning:** Kill a thousand, and a thousand more will come

**Club:** Queen's Park (Scotland)
**Motto:** *Ludere Causa Ludendi* (Latin)
**Meaning:** To play for the sake of playing

**Club:** Barcelona (Spain)
**Motto:** *Més que un club* (Catalan)
**Meaning:** More than a club

**Club:** Liverpool (England)
**Motto:** You'll Never Walk Alone

**Club:** Sporting Lisbon (Portugal)
**Motto:** *Esforço, Dedicação, Devoção, Glória* (Portuguese)
**Meaning:** Effort, dedication, devotion, glory

# BIG ARMS

Here are our versions of some really cool football badges from around the world to give you inspiration for making yours.

**Sampdoria (Italy)**: Sampdoria's shield includes an image of an old sailor called Baciccia, known as *lupo di mare* (wolf of the sea), with a pipe in his mouth. That's because Sampdoria are based in Genoa, Italy's biggest port city.

**Bohemians (Czech Republic)**: Bohemians have a green kangaroo on their badge because they toured Australia in 1927 and were given two kangaroos to take home. We don't think they were green though!

**Ajax (The Netherlands)**: Ajax have a drawing of the ancient Greek hero Ajax on their badge, who was known for his skills as a warrior. He is drawn with eleven separate lines to represent the eleven players in the team.

**Valencia (Spain)**: The Spanish city has a bat on its coat of arms and the football team has incorporated the same animal into its badge design. The bat opens its wings to wrap itself around the edge of the whole shield.

**Gent (Belgium)**: Gent call themselves The Buffalos, because in 1895 an American called Buffalo Bill visited Belgium with his circus. The audience chanted "Buffalo, buffalo!" during the show and the words stuck. Soon fans were chanting them at Gent's matches, which is how the club got their name.

And don't forget our coats of arms too:

## TERMS AND CONDITIONS APPLY

If you love your coat of arms, you might want to get it officially approved. The College of Arms, the official body which acts on powers given to them by the Crown, charges around £6,000 to grant you your own personal coat of arms. The College told us that no professional football clubs have ever been granted coats of arms. "Technically, their use of Arms is unlawful," they said. Naughty!

# ART QUIZ

**1. Who do you need to ask for official permission to use a coat of arms?**

a) The Arms Academy
b) The College of Arms
c) Arms R Us
d) Army McArmface

**2. What does the Latin phrase *Magnus frater spectat* te mean?**

a) Magnus farted while putting on his spectacles.
b) Big Brother is watching you.
c) You need to watch Magnus's brother.
d) Magnus's brother is watching you.

**3. What mythical creature is on the Liverpool club badge?**

a) Liverbird
b) Dragon
c) Unicorn
d) Yeti

**4. Which Argentine club, where Lionel Messi began his career, has a black and red badge with the letters N.O.B. on it?**

a) Nueva Olimpico Barracuda
b) Never Organize Birthdays
c) Neuquen Olimpo Brown
d) Newell's Old Boys

**5. What is the image on the badge of Italian team Roma?**

a) Gladiator Cassius Maximus fighting in the Colosseum
b) A she-wolf breast-feeding twins Romulus and Remus
c) A flight of doves
d) A soldier marching in a military parade

Friday
Lesson 5

# BUSINESS STUDIES

Earning money is difficult, but sometimes spending it is the hardest part.

It's like when Ben wants a new pair of trainers. He has the money in his pocket, but cannot decide which pair to buy. His mind is full of questions:

Ben must decide what he thinks is most important about his new pair of trainers, and weigh this up against the prices of the trainers in the shop. He must decide whether the shoes he wants are worth the money. This takes him ages and ages!

The same process takes place whenever we go shopping, whether it's for trainers, sweets, toys or cars. We ask ourselves: "Is this purchase worth the money?"

Today we'll talk about buying and selling footballers. We'll see how clubs decide who to buy and, once they decide, how they go about it.

Deal?

## THE PRICE IS RIGHT

When you buy a pint of milk, you know what you are getting: a pint of milk. You know that milk from one shop is the same as milk from another shop. You know that you need to drink it within a few days or it will go off. And you know that all pints of milk cost roughly the same.

Footballers are not like milk. All footballers are different and they are worth very different amounts of money. Here are some factors that determine the price of a player:

**International status:** If someone plays for their country, they will cost more. If a player has been capped for the national team it shows that they are one of the very best, which makes them more expensive.

**Age:** Players in their mid-20s are more expensive, because that's when most hit their best form. Very fast players may get slower as they get older.

**Position**: Strikers are often more expensive because they score the goals that make the difference between winning and losing. It is much harder to judge the true value of goalkeepers, which is why they tend to be the cheapest players.

**Celebrity status:** Sometimes clubs are not just thinking about performance, but also how famous the player is. A star player with charisma will increase interest in the team, which means that the club can earn more money on merchandising and sponsorship. Companies pay lots of money to be associated with celebrities. As a result, celebrity players often sell for higher amounts of money.

**Nationality:** Premier League rules state that teams have to have 8 players out of 25 who came through an English academy. That means there is a lot of competition to get the best English players, so they become more expensive. Also, players from countries with a rich football tradition, like Brazil or Argentina, often cost more than someone from, say, Malta or Zimbabwe, because it is more exciting having a Brazilian or an Argentine on your team.

# COMPLICATED CONTRACTS

Another reason why footballers are different from milk is that it is straightforward to buy a pint of milk. You pay the money and you get the milk, which belongs to you forever (until you pee it out).

When a club buys a footballer, the process is much more complicated. For a start, a club cannot buy a footballer forever. You buy them for a fixed amount of time, which will be stated in the **contract**, which is a piece of paper that sets out all the terms and conditions of the purchase. Both the player and the club must **sign** the contract, which is why we use the word "sign" when talking about footballers joining clubs. When a player joins a club, we can say that they signed for that club, or that the club has signed the player.

When a club signs a top player, they will try to sign that player for a long period of time to prevent a rival club from trying to buy them. Players nearing the end of their contracts are often much cheaper than players at the beginning or middle of their contracts, because at the end of the contract the selling club will no longer own the player and will therefore get nothing at all from a transfer.

## RISKY BUSINESS

Footballers are a high-risk purchase. You never know how a player will adapt to their new team. Players fail to adapt because they:

- Miss their family
- Receive different tactical demands
- Can't speak the language
- Don't like living in a new home
- Feel the weather is too cold/hot
- Get injured
- Are too busy partying

Sometimes the risk of buying an expensive player pays off. Real Madrid spent £80 million on Cristiano Ronaldo, a HUGE amount of money, but you never hear the fans complaining about his contribution to the club. He has helped them win two league titles and three Champions League titles, as well as smashing the all-time scoring record with over 400 goals for the team. And he's won four Ballon d'Or titles for the world's best player. He's almost a bargain!

### MOST EXPENSIVE PLAYERS IN THE WORLD

| PLAYER | DATE | FROM | TO | AMOUNT (€) |
|---|---|---|---|---|
| Paul Pogba | 2016 | Juventus | Manchester United | 89 million |
| Gareth Bale | 2013 | Tottenham Hotspur | Real Madrid | 85 million |
| Cristiano Ronaldo | 2009 | Manchester United | Real Madrid | 80 million |
| Gonzalo Higuain | 2016 | Napoli | Juventus | 75 million |
| Luis Suárez | 2014 | Liverpool | Barcelona | 65 million |

# HOW TO MAKE TRANSFERS STICK

A player moving from one club to another – usually when one is buying and the other is selling – is called a **transfer**. The process has several stages:

## 1. SCOUTING

A club looking for a new player comes up with a list of names. They will factor in position, age, speed, height, ability, budget and potential to improve. The club will have a shortlist of up to ten names and will start by trying to buy their first choice.

## 2. ENQUIRY

If a club is interested in a player who is under contract elsewhere, they need written permission from the player's current club to talk to him. Most players have an **agent**, who is the person who looks after their business affairs. Usually, the interested club gets in touch with the agent of their first-choice player, and will then make an official approach if the player is open to a move.

## 3. NEGOTIATIONS

Senior officials at the two clubs will negotiate a price, via email, text message or in person. Transfers can break down at this stage, because clubs have different valuations of players. The payment structure also has to be discussed: clubs might pay the whole sum upfront, but most pay in **instalments** over several periods, sometimes lasting years.

## 4. PERSONAL TERMS AND CLAUSES

The deal is not done until a contract is written up between the player and the new club. The contract includes details of how long the player will be at the club, their monthly salary, and any bonuses that may be due for games played, goals scored or trophies won. The buying club may also put in a **clause** – the word used by lawyers for a detail in the contract – that states that if the team is relegated they can reduce the salary.

## 5. MEDICAL

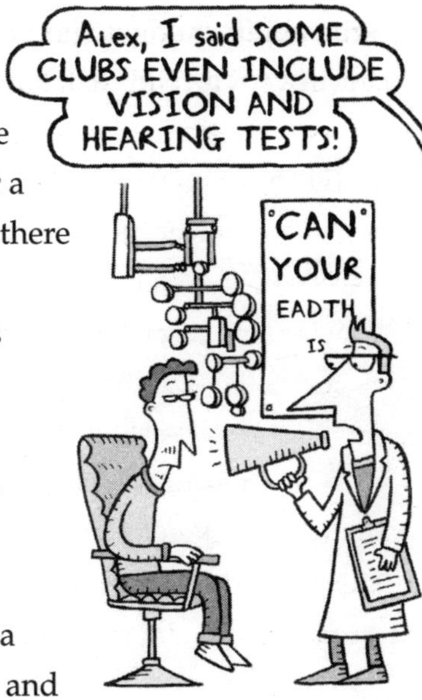


Before the deal is completed, the buying club will give the player a thorough medical to make sure there are no underlying injuries. A medical can take two days, as a player will have a full health check. The medical includes a comprehensive heart screening, and a check on the lower back and pelvic joints, which impact mobility. Goalkeepers have extra tests on their shoulders, elbows and wrists. Some clubs even include vision and hearing tests.

## 6. FINAL ADMIN

The transfer is complete once the details are registered with the FA or, for foreign players, with FIFA's Transfer Matching System database. In those cases, an ITC, short for International Transfer Certificate, is issued.

## ONE EXTRA SCOOP, PLEASE!

Sometimes it's not money that changes hands for a transfer.

### A FREEZER FULL OF ICE CREAM

**Hugh McLenahan, Stockport to Manchester United (1927)**

Selling club Stockport was holding a fund-raising event to ease its financial troubles and so United's assistant coach, Louis Rocca, whose family ran an ice cream business, sent two freezers full of ice cream in return for the defender. McLenahan played over 100 games and was even the United captain for a while. Chilly business!

### BODYWEIGHT IN PRAWNS

**Kenneth Kristensen, Vindbjart to Fløy (2002)**

What a great catch! Third division Norwegian club Fløy wanted to sign a striker from rivals Vindbjart, who decided that asking for the player's bodyweight in prawns would be a good deal. They played each other the following weekend: Kristensen weighed in at 165 pounds, and the deal was done. Shrimple!

### 30 TRACKSUITS

**Zat Knight, Rushall Olympic to Fulham (1999)**

Fulham made quite a profit on Knight, whom they bought from non-league side Rushall Olympic. They did not have to pay anything but owner Mohamed Al-Fayed sent 30 tracksuits by way of thanks. Knight ended up playing for England and was sold to Aston Villa for £3.5 million. Hope the trackies were nice!

# CLAUSE CONFUSION

Some contracts have very strange clauses:

**Player**: Spencer Prior
**Club**: Cardiff City
**Clause**: The player had to eat sheep's testicles after joining. Club owner Sam Hammam was a fun-loving businessman from Lebanon, where the food is a delicacy when served with a lemon and parsley sauce. Hammam added the clause for a laugh. Baaaaa-d!

**Player**: Mario Balotelli
**Club**: Liverpool
**Clause**: The Italian forward came with a reputation for misbehaving on the pitch, so was told that he would get a reward if he was sent off FEWER than four times in one season and did NOT spit on an opponent. He shouldn't be doing that anyway! He managed to behave. His reward? £1 million!

**Player**: Dennis Bergkamp
**Club**: Arsenal
**Clause**: Bergkamp insisted on a clause stating that he never needed to travel to away games by plane, since he was scared of flying.

**Player**: Stefan Schwarz
**Club**: Sunderland
**Clause**: Not allowed to fly into space. His agent had signed up for a flight on one of the first passenger flights into space, and the buying club was worried that he would take the Swedish midfielder with him. It never happened. And Schwarz got the nickname "Spaceman".

# BUSINESS STUDIES QUIZ

**1. Which player position usually goes for the least money in the transfer market?**

a) Goalkeeper
b) Defender
c) Midfielder
d) Striker

**2. According to his contract, what was Norwegian defender Stig Inge Bjørnebye forbidden from doing while a Liverpool player in the 1990s?**

a) Ski jumping
b) Fishing for trout
c) Painting
d) Scoring

**3. What does ITC stand for?**

a) Intense Transfer Confusion
b) Insane Transfer Contract
c) Immediate Transfer Clause
d) International Transfer Certificate

**4. Which player was Crystal Palace striker Christian Benteke especially pleased that his club signed in summer 2016?**

a) His uncle Steve Mandanda
b) His best friend Mathieu Flamini
c) His brother Jonathan Benteke
d) His hero Andros Townsend

**5. What was left-back Cohen Bramall's job before Arsenal signed him from seventh division side Hednesford Town in January 2017?**

a) Car factory worker
b) Fortune cookie writer
c) Gym personal trainer
d) Dog-surfing instructor

RECOVERY
AFTER SCHOOL CLUB

# SNOOZE-FEST

It's the end of the week, so time to reward yourself with some proper relaxation. Footballers need sleep and recovery time to perform at their best: they must sleep for the right amount of time and make sure they relax in the right way between games. This After School Club is all about how to relax – but you need to be switched on to know how to switch off!

Ben "The Pen" is Zen

## Relax 1: Keep it dark and cool

NINETY minutes before the time you want to fall asleep, switch off all electronic devices – phones, tablets, laptops. That's the same time as a football match! Make sure your bedroom is as dark as possible and keep it at a cool temperature.

---

**GOOD FOR: Achieving peak performance the next day**
**RECOVERY RATING: 1/4**

## Relax 2: Muscle love

You need to be lying in bed for this one. Take a deep breath, tense your toes and feet for a few seconds, and then breathe out slowly. Tighten your lower leg muscles for a few secs, release, then continue up the body: flex your upper legs, tummy area, lower back, chest and upper back, hands and arms.

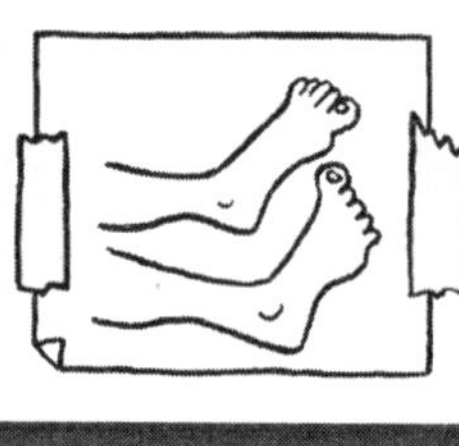

---

**GOOD FOR: Relieving tension in muscles**
**RECOVERY RATING: 2/4**

## Relax 3: Picture this

Think of something you really, really want. Maybe it is getting into the school football team, getting good marks for some homework or even baking a cake. Then think about all the steps you need to go through in order to achieve your goal. For each step, focus on the images in your mind. Sometimes imagining the step-by-step process of what you need to do – a technique called visualizing – can actually help that thing happen!

**GOOD FOR: Reducing anxiety, focusing on steps needed to reach goals**
**RECOVERY RATING: 3/4**

## Relax 4: 4-7-8 trick

This is a yoga exercise that experts think can make you fall asleep within one minute! Put the tip of your tongue just behind your upper front teeth and keep it there. Then take a big breath out through your mouth around your tongue. Close your mouth and breathe in quietly through your nose for 4 seconds. Hold your breath for 7 seconds. Exhale through your mouth for 8 seconds. Repeat 3 times. This exercise can take 2 months to perfect, but then you'll be counting the zzzzzzs in no time!

**GOOD FOR: Relaxing the body and staying calm**
**RECOVERY RATING: 4/4**

Breathe in ... two ... three ... four...
Hold breath ... two ... three ... four ... five ... six ... seven.
I love learning, but relaxing is nice too!
Having a rest is the perfect way to look back over all the new stuff we discovered this season.
I won't look at a ball the same way again!
I won't look at my pee the same way again!
How can I forget the team with kangaroos on its badge?
Or the one with a bat!

I now know which player was banned from flying into space!
The animal that's left-handed...
The stadium built in the shape of a crocodile...
What links William the Conqueror to football kits...
We've learned how to say football in more than twenty languages.
YOLO!
Breathe out ... two ... three ... four ... five ... six ... seven ... eight.
Sweet dreams everyone.
And see you back here for Football School Season 3!
Z Z Z Z Z
Z Z Z Z Z Z

# QUIZ ANSWERS

## PSHE
1. d
2. b
3. a
4. a
5. b

## MODERN LANGUAGES
1. b
2. c
3. c
4. a
5. c

## PHYSICS
1. d
2. c
3. c
4. a
5. c

## HISTORY
1. b
2. d
3. a
4. a
5. d

## GEOGRAPHY
1. b
2. d
3. d
4. a
5. b

## FILM STUDIES
1. b
2. a
3. b
4. d
5. b

## DESIGN AND TECHNOLOGY
1. d
2. d
3. b
4. c
5. c

## ENGLISH
1. a
2. c
3. b
4. a
5. c

## RELIGIOUS STUDIES
1. a
2. a (Gabriel Jesus and Jesus Navas)
3. b
4. d
5. c

## BIOLOGY
1. d
2. b
3. c
4. b
5. b

## MATHS
1. b
2. d
3. a
4. b
5. c

## PSYCHOLOGY
1. a
2. c
3. b
4. b
5. b

## ART
1. b
2. b
3. a
4. d
5. b

## BUSINESS STUDIES
1. a
2. a
3. d
4. c
5. a

# ACKNOWLEDGEMENTS

The winner of Football School's Man of the Match award goes to illustrator Spike Gerrell. He always scores when he draws!

The squad at Walker Books is brilliantly talented in strength and depth. We are grateful to captain Daisy "DJ" Jellicoe and her team-mates Denise Johnstone-Burt, Louise Jackson, Laurelie Bazin, Jenny Bish, Simon Armstrong, Alex Spears, Rosi Crawley and Kirsten Cozens.

Thanks again to our top notch backroom staff at Janklow & Nesbit, Rebecca Carter, Rebecca Folland and Kirsty Gordon, and at David Luxton Associates, David Luxton, Rebecca Winfield and Nick Walters.

We would like to thank the following experts for sharing their knowledge with us: Roma Agrawal, Duncan Alexander, Marcus Alves, Dr Anthony Bale, Jack Bates, Dr Lucja Biel, Charlie Brooks, Mads Burheim, Dr David Carey, Dr Mick Chappell, Peter Chipcase, Rhys Courtney, Michiel de Hoog, Wink de Putter, Taras Dolinsky, Dave Farrar, Caroline Federman, Daniel Geey, Manleen Gill, Gemma Gordon, Matt Grace, Jonathan Harding, Martyn Heather, Alex Holiga, Raphael Honigstein, Gary Hughes, Dr Paul Ibbotson, Motoko Jitsukawa, Uğur Karakullukçu, Sergio Krithinas, Christopher Lash, John Ledwidge, Ronnie Leyman, Ian Lynam, Karen Maxwell, Prof. Chris McManus, Steve McNally, Ben Miller, Mike Murphy at Steaditec, Venkat Nallamilli, Ben Oakley, Peter O'Donoghue, Rafael Ortega, Amanda Overend, Lauren Pearson, Tim Reeves, Emre Sarigul, Ionica Smeets, Harry Stopes, Prof. Stefan Szymanski, Benjamin Thompsett, David Winner, Nia Wyn Thomas, Michal Zachodny. Special thanks to Opta for all the data in the Maths lesson.

Cheers to our Star Pupils: Oscar Auerbach, Thomas Elks, Harry McAllester, Flora Pretor-Pinney, Ronnie Thomas-Armstrong and Cass Yechiel.

Ben would like to thank Annie for her inspiration and support, and Clemmy and Bibi for making him laugh every day and checking the jokes in this book are up to scratch.

Alex would like to thank Nat for being his family's star player, and Zak and Barnaby for the team hugs.

# ABOUT YOUR COACHES

**Alex Bellos** writes for the *Guardian* and has written several bestselling popular science books.

**Ben Lyttleton** is an author, broadcaster and consultant to professional football clubs.

**Spike Gerrell** draws cartoons for magazines and books.

# MORE FROM FOOTBALL SCHOOL

Subscribe on YouTube

**footballschool.co**

**youtube.com/FootballSchoolFacts**